MARY MAGDALEN

IN THE VISIONS OF
ANNE CATHERINE EMMERICH

"Mary therefore took a pound of ointment of right spikenard, of great price, and anointed the feet of Jesus, and wiped his feet with her hair, and the house was filled with the odour of the ointment."
—John 12:3

Mary Magdalen

MARY MAGDALEN

IN THE VISIONS OF
ANNE CATHERINE EMMERICH

Consisting of Excerpts from the 4-Volume
The Life of Jesus Christ and Biblical Revelations
From the Visions of
Anne Catherine Emmerich

"Mary hath chosen the best part,
which shall not be taken away
from her."   —Luke 10:42

TAN Books
Charlotte, North Carolina

Approbation for the excerpts from
The Life of Jesus Christ and Biblical Revelations:

NIHIL OBSTAT: IMPRÌMATUR:
Em. De Jaegher   A. C. De Schrevel
Can. lib. cens.   *Vic. Gen.*
Brugis, 14 Februarii 1914   Brugis, 14 Februarii 1914

Mary Magdalen in the Visions of Anne Catherine Emmerich (this selection and arrangement of the materials, plus the introductions) copyright © 2005 by TAN Books.

ISBN 978-0-89555-802-2

Front cover illustration: Photo of "St. Mary Magdalen" stained-glass window copyright © 1993 by Alan Brown. Used by arrangement with Al Brown Photo, 3597 N. Roberts Rd., Bardstown, Kentucky 40004.

This book is composed of selections from *The Life of Jesus Christ and Biblical Revelations: From the Visions of the Venerable Anne Catherine Emmerich as recorded in the journals of Clemens Brentano*, a 4-volume work which was arranged and edited by the Very Reverend Carl E. Schmöger, C.SS.R. and translated by an American nun, which English translation was published in 1914 by Desclée de Brouwer & Co. of Lille, Paris, and Bruges, in conjunction with the Sentinel Press of New York, and was republished by TAN Books in 1979, and then again with new type in 1986 and 2004. Section headings, section introductions and Appendices have been supplied by TAN Books.

Printed and bound in the United States of America.

TAN Books
Charlotte, North Carolina
www.TANBooks.com
2011

"And when Jesus was in Bethania, in the house of Simon the leper, there came to him a woman having an alabaster box of precious ointment, and poured it on his head as he was at table. And the disciples seeing it, had indignation, saying: To what purpose is this waste? For this might have been sold for much, and given to the poor. And Jesus knowing *it*, said to them: Why do you trouble this woman? for she hath wrought a good work upon me. For the poor you have always with you: but me you have not always. For she in pouring this ointment upon my body, hath done it for my burial.

"Amen I say to you, wheresoever this gospel shall be preached in the whole world, that also which she hath done, shall be told for a memory of her."

—*Matthew* 26:10-13

Contents

Appendices

1. The Family of Lazarus, Martha and Magdalen

The parents of Lazarus had in all fifteen children, of whom six died young. Of the nine that survived, only four were living at the time of Christ's teaching. These four were: Lazarus; Martha, about two years younger; Mary, looked upon as a simpleton, two years younger than Martha; and Mary Magdalen, five years younger than the simpleton. The simpleton is not named in Scripture, not reckoned among the Lazarus family; but she is known to God. She was always put aside in her family, and lived altogether unknown. . . .

Lazarus . . . looked much older than Jesus; he appeared to me to be fully eight years His senior. Lazarus had large possessions, landed property, gardens, and many servants. Martha had her own house, and another sister named Mary, who lived entirely alone, had also her separate dwelling. Magdalen lived in her castle at Magdalum. Lazarus was already long acquainted with the Holy Family. He had at an early period aided Joseph and Mary with large alms and, from first to last, did much for the Community. The purse that Judas carried and all the early expenses, he supplied out of his own wealth. . . .

The father of Lazarus was named Zarah, or Zerah, and was of very noble Egyptian descent. He had dwelt in Syria, on the confines of Arabia, where he held a position under the Syrian king; but for services rendered in war, he received from the Roman emperor property near

1

Jerusalem and in Galilee. He was like a prince, and was very rich. He had acquired still greater wealth by his wife Jezabel, a Jewess of the sect of the Pharisees. He became a Jew, and was pious and strict according to the Pharisaical laws. He owned part of the city on Mount Zion, on the side upon which the brook near the height on which the Temple stands, flows through the ravine. But the greater part of this property, he had bequeathed to the Temple, retaining, however, in his family some ancient privilege on its account. This property was on the road by which the Apostles went up to the Cenacle, but the Cenacle itself formed no longer a part of it. Zarah's castle in Bethania was very large. It had numerous gardens, terraces, and fountains, and was surrounded by double ditches. The prophecies of Anna and Simeon were known to the family of Zarah, who were waiting for the Messiah. Even in Jesus' youth, they were acquainted with the Holy Family, just as pious, noble people are wont to be with their humble, devout neighbors.   (Vol. 1, pp. 334-335)

2. Magdalen's Childhood

Magdalen, the youngest child, was very beautiful and, even in her early years, tall and well-developed like a girl of more advanced age. She was full of frivolity and seductive art. Her parents died when she was only seven years old. She had no great love for them even from her earliest age, on account of their severe fasts. Even as a child, she was vain beyond expression, given to petty thefts, proud, self-willed, and a lover of pleasure. She was never faithful, but clung to whatever flattered her the most. She was, therefore, extravagant in her pity when her sensitive compassion was aroused, and kind and condescending to all that appealed to her senses by some external show. Her mother had had some share in Magdalen's faulty education, and that sympathetic softness the child had inherited from her.

Magdalen was spoiled by her mother and her nurse. They showed her off everywhere, caused her cleverness and pretty little ways to be admired, and sat much with her dressed up at the window. That window-sitting was the chief cause of her ruin. I saw her at the window and on the terraces of the house upon a magnificent seat of carpets and cushions, where she could be seen in all her splendor from the street. She used to steal sweetmeats, and take them to other children in the garden of the castle. Even in her ninth year she was engaged in love affairs.

With her developing talents and beauty, increased also the talk and admiration they excited. She had crowds of companions. She was taught, and she wrote love verses on little rolls of parchment. I saw her while so engaged counting on her fingers. She sent these verses around, and exchanged them with her lovers. Her fame spread on all sides, and she was exceedingly admired.

But I never saw that she either really loved or was loved. It was all, on her part at least, vanity, frivolity, self-adoration, and confidence in her own beauty. I saw her a scandal to her brother and sisters whom she despised and of whom she was ashamed on account of their simple life.

(Vol. 1, pp. 335-336)

---

3. Magdalen Inherits the Castle of Magdalum

When the patrimony was divided, the castle of Magdalum fell by lot to Magdalen. It was a very beautiful building. Magdalen had often gone there with her family when she was a very young child, and she had always entertained a special preference for it. She was only about eleven years old when, with a large household of servants, men and maids, she retired thither and set up a splendid establishment for herself.

Magdalum was a fortified place, consisting of several castles, public buildings and large squares of groves and gardens. It was eight hours east of Nazareth, about three from Capharnaum, one and a half from Bethsaida toward the south, and about a mile from the Lake of Genesareth. It was built on a slope of the mountain and extended down into the valley which stretches off toward the lake and around its shores. One of those castles belonged to Herod. He possessed a still larger one in the fertile region of Genesareth. Some of his soldiers were stationed in Magdalum, and they contributed their share to the general demoralization. The officers were on intimate terms with Magdalen. There were, besides the troops, about two hundred people in Magdalum, chiefly officials, master builders, and servants.

The castle of Magdalum was the highest and most magnificent of all; from its roof one could see across the Sea of Galilee to the opposite shore. Five roads led to Magdalum, and on every one at one half-hour's distance from the well-fortified place, stood a tower built over an arch. It was like a watchtower whence could be seen far into the distance. These towers had no connection with one another; they rose out of a country covered with gardens, fields, and meadows. Magdalen had men servants and maids, fields and herds, but a very disorderly household; all went to rack and ruin.   (Vol. 1, pp. 336-337)

4. Magdalen's Reputation

*Sts. Zachary and Elizabeth being long since dead,
St. John the Baptist has been preaching and
baptizing publicly and is gaining fame and followers.
Jesus has just begun His public life,
but is yet to perform any miracles.**

Six men who were coming from the baptism of John met Jesus. Among them were Levi, known later as Matthew, and two sons of the widowed relatives of Elizabeth. They all knew Jesus, some through relationship, others by hearsay; and they strongly suspected, though they had had no assurance of it, that He was the One of whom John had spoken. They spoke of John, of Lazarus and his sisters, especially of Magdalen. They supposed she had a devil, for she was already living apart from her family in the castle of Magdalum. These men accompanied Jesus, and were filled with astonishment at His discourse. The aspirants to baptism going from Galilee to John used to tell him all that they knew and heard of Jesus, while they that came from Ainon, where John baptized, used to tell Jesus all they knew of John. . . . Magdalen's castle in Magdalum was not far off, and Magdalen herself was at this time at the height of her glory.   (Vol. 1, pp. 342, 352)

5. Jesus Speaks of Magdalen's Family

Lazarus had three sisters: the eldest Martha, the youngest Mary Magdalen, and one between them also called Mary. This last lived altogether secluded, her silence causing her to be looked upon as a simpleton. She

---

*In most cases we have provided introductions for sections which do not follow immediately upon the preceding section. —*Publisher*, 2005.

went by no other name than Silent Mary. Jesus, speaking to Eliud of this family, said, "Martha is good and pious. She will, with her brother, follow Me." Of Mary the Silent, He said, "She is possessed of great mind and understanding; but, for the good of her soul, they have been withdrawn from her. She is not for this world, therefore is she now altogether secluded from it. But she has never committed sin. If I should speak to her, she would perfectly comprehend the greatest mysteries. She will not live much longer. After her death, Lazarus and his sister Martha will follow me and devote all that they possess to the use of the Community. The youngest sister Mary has strayed from the right path, but she will return and rise to higher sanctity than Martha."

Jesus . . . spoke of Lazarus by another general name, which I have forgotten. He mentioned also his father, saying that he had been in war. He said that Lazarus and his sisters were rich, and that they would devote all they had to the advancement of Redemption.   (Vol. 1, pp. 374-375)

---

6. Martha Speaks to Jesus about Magdalen

Jesus now has a large group of followers and is on His way to the place of Baptism. He is welcomed to Martha's castle in Bethania where she and her brother Lazarus live, along with their sister Silent Mary.

No word had as yet been spoken in Jesus' presence in reference to Magdalen, who was then living at Magdalum in the height of her grandeur. . . .

Martha spoke to Jesus of Magdalen and her own great anxiety on her account. Jesus comforted her, telling her that Magdalen would certainly be converted, but that she must on no account weary of praying for her and exhorting her to change her life.   (Vol. 1. pp. 401, 404)

7. How Silent Mary Lived

Jesus said of Silent Mary: "She is not without understanding, but her soul is not of this world. She sees not this world, and this world comprehends her not. She is happy. She knows no sin."

Silent Mary, the simple sister of Lazarus, did not make her appearance. Before others she never uttered a word; but when alone in her room or the garden, she talked aloud to herself and to all the objects around her, as if they had life. It was only before others that she was perfectly mute and still; her eyes cast down, she looked like a statue. On being saluted, however, she inclined and was very polite in all her bearing. When alone, she busied herself in various occupations, attending to her own wardrobe, and keeping all things in order. She was very pious, though she never appeared in the school. She prayed in her own chamber. I think she had visions and conversed with apparitions. Her love for her brother and sisters was unspeakable, especially for Magdalen. From her earliest years she had been what she now was. She had a female attendant, but she was perfectly neat in her person and surroundings with no trace of insanity to be found about her.

She prayed most piously and devoutly, and endured a kind of expiatory suffering for the sins of others, for her soul was often oppressed as if the weight of the whole world was upon her. Her dwelling was comfortably fitted up with sofas and different kinds of furniture. She ate little and always alone. She died of grief at the immensity of Jesus' Passion, which in spirit she foresaw.

(Vol. 1, pp. 400, 401, 404)

8. Silent Mary's Prophecy

Jesus had an interview with the women in a chamber
fronting on the road that led to Jerusalem, and which had
formerly been occupied by Magdalen. In obedience to
Jesus' direction, Lazarus brought his silent sister Mary
and left her alone with the Lord, the other women retiring
in the meantime to the antechamber.

Silent Mary . . . cast herself down before Him and
kissed His feet. Jesus made no attempt to prevent her, and
raised her up by the hand. With her eyes turned heaven-
ward, she uttered the most sublime and wonderful things,
though in the most simple and natural manner. She spoke
of God, of His Son, and of His Kingdom just as a peasant
girl might talk of the father of the village lord and his
inheritance. Her words were a prophecy, and the things of
which she spoke she saw before her. She recounted the
grave faults and bad management of the wicked servants
of the household. The Father had sent His Son to arrange
affairs and pay off all debts, but they would receive Him
badly. He would have to die in great suffering, redeem His
Kingdom with His own Blood, and efface the crimes of the
servants, that they might again become the children of
His Father. She carried out the allegory in most beautiful
language, and yet in as natural a manner as if she were
recounting a scene enacted in her presence. At times she
was gay, at others sorrowful, calling herself a useless servant and grieving over the painful labors of the Son of the
merciful Lord and Father. Another cause of sorrow to her
was that the servants would not rightly understand the
parable, although so simple and so true. She spoke of the
Resurrection. The Son, she said, would go to the servants
in the subterranean prisons also. He would console them
and set them free, because He had purchased their
Redemption. He would return with them to His Father.

But at His second advent, when He would come again to judge, all those that had abused the satisfaction He had made and who would not turn from their evil ways, should be cast into the fire. She then spoke of Lazarus' death and resurrection: "He goes forth from this world," she said, "and gazes upon the things of the other life. His friends weep around him as if he were never to return. But the Son calls him back to earth, and he labors in the vineyard." Of Magdalen too she spoke: "The maiden is in the frightful desert where once were the children of Israel. She wanders in accursed places where all is dark, where never human foot has trod. But she will come forth, and in another desert make amends for the past."

(Vol. 1, pp. 484-485)

---

9. At the End of Jesus' Forty Days Fast

Jesus has been baptized by John the Baptist, after which He and His disciples travel through Judea. He cures many ill and allows His disciples to baptize those unable to travel to see John. He tells His disciples that He will retire for awhile and tells Lazarus that He will return in forty days. Alone and barefooted, He heads into the desert, where He fasts and prays and conquers every temptation, reaffirming His decision to suffer and die for the salvation of the world. At the end of the forty days, He is refreshed by spiritual food and drink brought by angels.

The angels that ministered unto Jesus appeared under different forms and seemed to belong to different hierarchies. Those that, at the close of the banquet, bore away the cups of wine and morsels of bread, were clothed in priestly raiment. I saw at the instant of their disappearance, all kinds of supernatural consolation descending upon the friends of Jesus, those of His own time and those

of after ages. I saw Jesus appearing in vision to the
Blessed Virgin then at Cana, to comfort and strengthen
her. I saw Lazarus and Martha wonderfully touched,
while their hearts grew warm with the love of Jesus. I saw
Mary the Silent actually fed with the gifts from the table
of the Lord. The angel stood by her while she, like a child,
received the food. She had been a witness of all the temptation and sufferings of Jesus. Her whole life was one of
visions and suffering through compassion, therefore such
supernatural favors caused her no astonishment. Magdalen, too, was wonderfully agitated. She was at the time
busied with finery for some amusement. Suddenly, anxiety about her life seized upon her, and a longing rose in
her soul to be freed from the chains that bound her. She
cast the finery from her hands, but was laughed at by
those around her. I saw many of the future Apostles consoled, their hearts filled with heavenly desires. . . . Peter,
Andrew, and all the others were, as I saw, strengthened
and consoled. This was a most wonderful vision.

(Vol. 2, pp. 18-19)

10. Magdalen's First Attempt to See Jesus

Jesus returns from the desert and is quickly rejoined
by many of His disciples, who begin again to baptize.
He is invited to the marriage feast at Cana, where
He performs His first public miracle. He and His
disciples travel in the area around the Sea of Galilee.

A couple of hours from Gadara, Jesus again crossed the
Jordan, and went on toward the southwest, leaving Scyth-
opolis to the left. He crossed Mount Moreh to Jezrael, a
city on the west side of the plain Esdrelon. Jesus cured
numbers there openly before the synagogue. But He
stayed a few hours only in Jezrael, so that Magdalen who,

at the earnest entreaty of Martha, had come with her to see Jesus, did not find Him on her arrival. She heard only of His miracles from the lips of those whom He had cured. The sisters here separated, and Magdalen retraced her steps to Magdalum. . . . Jesus consoled Lazarus on the subject of Magdalen, of whom He said that already there had fallen upon her soul a spark of salvation, which would entirely consume her.   (Vol. 2, pp. 64, 72)

11. Magdalen's First Call to Conversion

Jesus and His disciples travel to Galilee, where He continues teaching and performing miracles. John the Baptist is now no longer baptizing but is preaching of Jesus and referring all who ask for baptism to the disciples of Jesus.

Jesus taught in Jezrael and performed many miracles before a great concourse of people. All the disciples from Galilee were here assembled to meet Him. Nathanael Chased, Nathanael the bridegroom, Peter, James, John, the sons of Mary Cleophas, all were there. Lazarus, Martha, Seraphia (Veronica) and Johanna Chusa, who had come before from Jerusalem, had visited Magdalen at her castle of Magdalum to persuade her to go with them to Jezrael in order to see, if not to hear, the wise, the admirable, the most eloquent, and most beautiful Jesus, of whom the whole country was full. Magdalen had yielded to the persuasions of the women and, surrounded by much vain display, accompanied them thither. As she stood at the window of an inn gazing down into the street, Jesus and His disciples came walking by. He looked at her gravely as He passed, with a glance that pierced her soul. An unusual feeling of confusion came over her. Violently agitated, she rushed from the inn and, impelled by an overpowering sense of her own misery, hid in a house wherein lepers and women afflicted with bloody flux found a refuge. It was a kind of hospital under the superintendence of a Pharisee. The people of the inn from which Magdalen had fled, knowing the life she was leading, cried out: "That's the right place for her, among lepers and people tormented with bloody flux!"

But Magdalen had fled to the house of the leprous through that feeling of intense humiliation roused in her soul by the glance of Jesus, for she had made her way into that respectable position among the other women through a motive of pride, not wishing to stand in the crowd of poor, common people. Accompanied by Lazarus, she returned to Magdalum with Martha and the other women. The next Sabbath was there celebrated by them, for Magdalum could boast a synagogue.   (Vol. 2, pp. 78-79)

12. Jesus Reassures Martha

Jesus continues performing miracles and exorcisms before ever-increasing crowds in Capharnaum.

In the evening Jesus went to His Mother's house between Bethsaida and Capharnaum, whither had come Lazarus with Martha and the other women from Jerusalem. They were on their way from Magdalum and had called to take leave of Mary before returning to Jerusalem. He said that Martha was too anxious, that Magdalen had been very deeply affected, yet she would, notwithstanding, relapse once more into her old ways. She had not yet laid aside her fine attire, for, as she declared, one in her position could not dress so plainly as the other women, etc.   (Vol. 2, pp. 80-81)

13. Lazarus' Villa

*Jesus and His disciples travel to many cities
in Galilee, where they are met by crowds so
large that the people have to be held back
in order for Jesus to pass. He gains many new
followers by His teachings and His many miraculous
cures. The number of John the Baptist's disciples has
diminished and Herod now visits him regularly.*

Proceeding on His journey, He was met by Lazarus, John Marc, and Obed, who had come for that purpose. With them Jesus went on to Lazarus' villa near Thirza, about five hours distant. They arrived unnoticed and by night, and found all things ready for their reception. The villa was on a mountain toward Samaria, not far from Jacob's field. A very old Jew, who went barefoot and girt, was the steward, an office he had held even when Mary and Joseph stopped here on their journey to Bethlehem. It was at this same villa that Martha and Magdalen, in Jesus' last year when He was teaching in Samaria, showed Him hospitality and implored Him to come to their brother Lazarus who was sick.

Near that estate of Lazarus was the then small city of Thirza, situated in a lovely region about seven hours' journey from Samaria. The morning sun, to which Thirza was exposed, rendered it extremely fruitful in grain, wine and orchard fruits. The inhabitants were engaged chiefly in agriculture, the products of which they carried to a distance for sale. The city was once large and handsome and the residence of kings, but the palace had been consumed by fire and the city ruined by war. One king, Amri, had made that property of Lazarus his home until the building of Samaria, whither he then removed. The people of Thirza were in Jesus' time very pious and lived very retired in their little, isolated city. . . . Jesus taught in the synagogue of Thirza, but performed no cures.

(Vol. 2, pp. 102-103)

---

14. Magdalen Is the Lost Pearl

*Jesus celebrates the Pasch in Jerusalem, at which time
He turns the vendors and merchants out of the Temple.
Mary the Silent dies in the presence of the Blessed Virgin
and the holy women in Bethania. Herod has John the
Baptist arrested for speaking out too forcefully against
Herod's unlawful union with Herodias (his brother's
wife). While in prison, John is visited by his disciples,
whom he tells to leave him and follow Jesus. Jesus and
His disciples visit Lazarus and Martha in Bethania,
who offer to establish inns for use on their journeys,
since many Jews, under the influence of the Pharisees,
will provide them with nothing.*

While Jesus was walking up and down the hall with the
men, the women sat playing a kind of lottery for the benefit of their new undertaking. On the elevated platform
was a table on rollers, around which they sat. The plane of
the table, which projected into five angles like the rays of
a star, covered a box about two inches in depth. From the
five points to the center of this partitioned box, ran deep
furrows on the surface, and between them were slits con-
necting the interior. Each of the women had some long
strings of pearls and many other little precious stones.
Each in turn placed some of them in one of the furrows on
the table. Then resting a delicate little bow on the outer
end of the furrow, she shot a tiny arrow at the nearest
pearl or stone. The shock received by this one communi-
cated itself to the rest, which rolled into the other furrows
or dropped through the holes into the compartments in
the interior of the box. When all the pearls and stones had

been shot from the surface, the table, which was upon rollers, was agitated to and fro, by which movement the contents fell into other little compartments which could be drawn out at the edge. Each of these little drawers had previously been assigned to one of the players, so that when the holy women drew them out, they saw at once what they had won for their new undertaking, or which jewel they had lost.

During the game the holy women lost a very precious pearl that had fallen down among them. All moved back and looked for it most carefully. When at last they found it and were expressing their joy, Jesus came over to them and related the parable of the lost drachma and the joy of the owner upon finding it again. From their pearl, lost, carefully sought, and joyfully found, He drew a new similitude to Magdalen. He called her a pearl more precious than many others that, from the lottery table of holy love, had fallen and were going to destruction. "With what joy," He exclaimed, "will ye find again the precious pearl!" Then the women, deeply moved, asked: "Ah, Lord! Will that pearl be found again?" and Jesus answered: "Seek ye more earnestly than the woman in the parable sought the lost drachma, or the shepherd his stray sheep." Profoundly touched at this answer, all promised to seek after Magdalen more diligently than after their lost pearl, and assured Him that their joy upon finding her would far exceed what they now felt.

(Vol. 2, pp. 174-175)

15. Dina (The Woman at the Well)

With some of His disciples, Jesus travels to Samaria
where He meets Dina at Jacob's Well. He invites her
and all of Samaria to be reconciled with God.
He tells Dina of many ways in which she can
do penance and how she can repair her scandals.

Dina was an intelligent woman of some standing in the
world, the offspring of a mixed marriage, a Jewish mother
and a pagan father, born upon a country seat near Damascus. She had lost her parents at an early age, and had
been cared for by a dissolute nurse, by whom her evil passions had been fostered. She had had five husbands, one
after another. Some had died of grief, others had been put
out of the way by her new lovers. She had three daughters
and two half-grown sons, all of whom had remained with
the relatives of their respective fathers when their mother
was obliged to leave Damascus . . .

The man with whom she was now living was a relative
of one of her former husbands. He was a rich merchant.
As Dina followed the Samaritan religion, she had
induced the man to remove to Sichar, where she super-
intended his household and lived with him, though without being espoused to him. They were looked upon in
Sichar as a married couple. The husband was a vigorous
man of about thirty-six years with a ruddy face and a
reddish beard. There were many things in Dina's life
similar to those of Magdalen's, but she had fallen more
deeply than the latter. Still, I once saw that in the beginning of Magdalen's evil career at Magdalum, one of her
lovers lost his life at the hand of a rival. Dina was an
uncommonly gifted, open-hearted, easily influenced,
pleasing woman of great vivacity and impetuosity, but
she was always disturbed in conscience. She was living
now more respectably, that is, with this, her reputed hus-

band, in a house that stood alone and surrounded by a moat, near the gate leading from Sichar to the spring house. Though not held in contempt by the inhabitants, still they did not have much communication with her. Her manners were different from theirs, her costume elaborate and studied, all which, however, they pardoned in her as she was a stranger. . . . Dina's sons at a later period joined the seventy-two disciples.

(Vol. 2, pp. 188-189)

---

16. A Possessed Woman in Suphan (The Suphanite)

The Pharisees have become more bold in speaking out against Jesus and in trying to ensnare Him in a contradiction. He heals the Centurion's son. John the Baptist is interrogated by Herod, who offers to set him free if he will stop preaching against Herod's adultery. John refuses and is moved into a cell with no communication with his followers. Because of the multitude of sick in the city of Bezech, Jesus tells Andrew, John and Judas Barsabas to go and cure some of them in His name; they do so. He then travels to Suphan, where He is greeted with respect by the Pharisees of that city. He teaches and cures many ill.

While Jesus was busy curing the sick, a beautiful woman of middle age and in the garb of a stranger entered the large portico by the gate leading from the city. Her head and hair were wound in a thin veil woven with pearls. She wore a bodice in shape somewhat like a heart, and open at the sides, something like a scapular thrown over the head and fastened together around the body by straps reaching from the back. Around the neck and breast it was ornamented with cords and pearls.

From it fell, in folds to the ankle, two deep skirts, one shorter than the other. Both were of fine white wool embroidered with large, colored flowers. The sleeves were wide and fastened with armlets. To the shoulder straps that connected the front and back of the bodice was attached the upper part of a short mantle that fell over the arms. Over this flowed a long veil, of the whiteness of wool.

The woman, ashamed and anxious, entered slowly and timidly, her pale countenance bespeaking confusion and her eyes red from weeping. She wanted to approach Jesus, but the crowd was so great that she could not get near Him. The Pharisees keeping order went to her, and she at once addressed them: "Lead me to the Prophet, that He may forgive my sins and cure me!" The Pharisees stopped her with the words: "Woman, go home! What do you want here? The Prophet will not speak to you. How can He forgive you your sins? He will not busy Himself with you, for you are an adulteress." When the woman heard these words, she grew pale, her countenance assumed a frightful expression, she threw herself on the ground, rent her mantle from top to bottom, snatched her veil from her head and cried: "Ah, then I am lost! Now they lay hold of me! They are tearing me to pieces! See, there they are!" and she named five devils who were raging against her, one of her husband, the other four of her paramours. It was a fearful spectacle. Some of the women standing around raised her from the ground, and bore her wailing to her home. Jesus knew well what was going on, but He would not put the Pharisees of this place to shame. He did not interfere, but quietly continued His work of healing, for her hour had not yet come.   (Vol. 2, pp. 312-314)

17. Jesus Heals Mary the Suphanite

*Jesus and His disciples go with the Pharisees toward
a public hall, where a feast has been prepared for them.
On the way Jesus asks where the woman whom they sent
away from Him in the morning lives. Jesus leaves His
companions and enters her house through the courtyard.*

As Jesus approached . . . the devil, who had possession of
her, drove her from one corner to another. She was like a
timorous animal that would hide itself. As Jesus was traversing the court and drawing near to where she was, she
fled through a corridor and into a cellar in the side of the
hill upon which her house was built. In it was a vessel like
a great cask, narrow above and wide below. She wanted to
hide herself in it, but when she tried to do so, it burst with
a loud crash. It was an immense earthen vessel. Jesus
meantime halted and cried: "Mary of Suphan . . . I command thee in the Name of God to come to Me!" Then the
woman, enveloped from head to foot, as if the demons
forced her still to hide in her mantle, came creeping to
Jesus' feet on all fours, like a dog awaiting the whip. But
Jesus said to her: "Stand up!" She obeyed, but drew her veil
tightly over her face and around her neck as if she wanted
to strangle herself. Then said the Lord to her: "Uncover thy
face!" and she unwound her veil, but lowering her eyes and
averting them from Jesus as if forced to do so by an interior power. Jesus, approaching His head to hers, said:
"Look at Me!" and she obeyed. He breathed upon her, a
black vapor went out of her on all sides, and she fell unconscious before Him. Her servant maids, alarmed by the loud
bursting of the cask, had hurried thither and were standing nearby. Jesus directed them to take their mistress
upstairs and lay her on a bed. He soon followed with two of
the disciples that had accompanied Him, and found her
weeping bitter tears. He went to her, laid His hand on her

head, and said: "Thy sins are forgiven thee!" She wept
vehemently and sat up. And now her three children
entered the room, a boy about twelve years old, and two little girls of about nine and seven. The girls wore little short-
sleeved tunics embroidered in yellow. Jesus stepped
forward to meet the children, spoke to them kindly, asked
them some questions, and gave them some instruction.
Their mother said: "Thank the Prophet! He has cured me!"
whereupon the little ones fell on the ground at Jesus' feet.
He blessed them, led them one by one to their mother, in
order of age, and put their little hands into hers.

Jesus went into the entertainment hall in which were
the Pharisees and the rest of the disciples, and took His
place with them at table. The Pharisees were somewhat
displeased that Jesus had left them and gone to seek the
woman whom they had so harshly repulsed that morning
before so many people. But they said nothing, fearing to
receive a reproof themselves. Jesus treated them with
much consideration during the meal, and taught in
numerous similitudes and parables. Toward the middle of
the entertainment, the three children of the Suphanite
entered in their holiday dresses. One of the little girls bore
an urn full of odoriferous water, the other had a similar
one of nard, and the boy carried a vessel. They entered the
hall by the door opposite the unoccupied side of the table,
cast themselves down before Jesus, and set their presents
on the table in front of Him. Mary herself followed with
her maids, but she dared not approach. She was veiled,
and carried a shining crystal vase with colored veins like
marble in which, surrounded by upright sprays of delicate
green foliage, were various kinds of costly aromatics. Her
children had offered similar vases, but smaller. The Pharisees cast forbidding glances upon the mother and children. But Jesus said: "Draw near, Mary!" and she stepped
humbly behind Him, while her children, to whom she had

handed it, deposited her offering beside the others on the table. Jesus thanked her. The Pharisees murmured as later on they did at Magdalen's present to Jesus. They thought it a great waste, quite opposed to economy and compassion for the needy; however, they only wanted something to bring against the poor woman. Jesus spoke to her very kindly, as also to the children, to whom He presented some fruit which they took away with them. The Suphanite remained veiled and standing humbly behind Jesus. He said to the Pharisees: "All gifts come from God. For precious gifts, gratitude gives in return what it has the most precious, and that is no waste. The people that gather and prepare these spices must live." Then He directed one of the disciples to give the value of them to the poor, spoke some words upon the woman's conversion and repentance, restored her to the good opinion of all, and called upon the inhabitants of the city to treat her affectionately. Mary spoke not a word, but wept quietly under her veil the whole time. At last she cast herself in silence at Jesus' feet, rose, and left the dining hall.(Vol. 2, pp. 315-318)

18. Magdalen's Interior Struggle

From Suphan Jesus travels to many other cities in the region, teaching against idolatry and converting many pagans, who joyously embrace His teachings. Everywhere the sick gather in crowds to see Him, hoping to be cured. Judas is presented to Him as one desirous of becoming a disciple, and Jesus accepts his request. There is now a small number of people who have given up everything to follow Jesus.

During the healing of the sick, Manahem, the blind disciple of Korea, who had been restored to sight and whom

Jesus had sent on a message to Lazarus, returned from Bethania with the two nephews of Joseph of Arimathea. Jesus gave them an interview. The holy women had sent by them money and gifts of various kinds to Jesus. Dina the Samaritan had visited the holy women at Capharnaum, bringing with her a rich contribution. Veronica and Joanna Chusa had also visited Mary. On their return journey they called to see Magdalen, whom they found very much changed. She was depressed in spirits, her folly apparently undergoing a struggle with her good inclinations.   (Vol. 2, p. 428)

19. Martha Invites Magdalen to Go and Hear Jesus

Jesus meets Judas' family in Iscariot, who receive Him cordially. From there He and His disciples travel northward to Mount Gabara, visiting many cities along the way. Jesus sends His disciples ahead of Him into the surrounding area to tell the people that He will be giving a great instruction on the mount. The people gather in great numbers, bringing with them their sick of all kinds.

Magdalen also wended her way to the mount of instruction near Gabara. Martha and Anna Cleophas had left Damna, where the holy women had an inn, and gone to Magdalum with the view of persuading Magdalen to attend the sermon that Jesus was about to deliver on the mountain beyond Gabara. Veronica, Johanna Chusa, Dina, and the Suphanite had meanwhile remained at Damna, distant three hours from Capharnaum and over one hour from Magdalum. Magdalen received her sister in a manner rather kind and showed her into an apartment not far from her room of state, but into this latter she did not take her. There was in Magdalen a mixture of true and false shame. She was partly ashamed of her simple, pious, and plainly dressed sister who went around with Jesus' followers so despised by her visitors and associates, and she was partly ashamed of herself before Martha. It was this feeling that prevented her taking the latter into the apartments that were the scenes of her follies and vices. Magdalen was somewhat broken in spirits, but she lacked the courage to disengage herself from her surroundings. She looked pale and languid. The man with whom she lived, on account of his low and vulgar sentiments, was utterly distasteful to her.

Martha treated her very prudently and affectionately. She said to her: "Dina and Mary, the Suphanite, whom you know, two amiable and clever women, invite you to be present with them at the instruction that Jesus is going to give on the mountain. It is so near, and they are so anxious for your company. You need not be ashamed of them before the people, for they are respectable, they dress with taste, and they have distinguished manners. You will behold a very wonderful spectacle: the crowds of people, the marvelous eloquence of the Prophet, the sick, the cures that He effects, the hardihood with which He addresses the Pharisees! Veronica, Mary Chusa, and Jesus' Mother, who wishes you so well—we all are convinced that you will thank us for the invitation. I think it will cheer you up a little. You appear to be quite forlorn here, you have no one around you who can appreciate your heart and your talents. Oh, if you would only pass some time with us in Bethania! We hear so many wonderful things, and we have so much good to do, and you have always been so full of compassion and kindness. You must at least come to Damna with me tomorrow morning. There you will find all the women of our party at the inn. You can have a private apartment and meet only those that you know," etc. In this strain Martha spoke to her sister, carefully avoiding anything that might wound her. Magdalen's sadness predisposed her to listen favorably to Martha's proposals. She did indeed raise a few difficulties, but at last yielded and promised Martha to accompany her to Damna. She took a repast with her and went several times during the evening from her own apartments to see her. Martha and Anna Cleophas prayed together that night that God would render the coming journey fruitful in good for Magdalen.

A few days previously James the Greater, impelled by a feeling of intense compassion for Magdalen, had come to invite her to the preaching soon to take place at Gabara. She had received him at a neighboring house. James was in appearance very imposing. His speech was grave and full of wisdom, though at the same time most pleasing. He made a most favorable impression upon Magdalen, and she received him graciously whenever he was in that part of the country. James did not address to her words of reproof; on the contrary, his manner toward her was marked by esteem and kindliness, and he invited her to be present at least once at Jesus' preaching. It would be impossible, he said, to see or hear one superior to Him. She had no need to trouble herself about the other auditors, and she might appear among them in her ordinary dress. Magdalen had received his invitation favorably, but she was still undecided as to whether she should or should not accept it, when Martha and Anna Cleophas arrived.

(Vol. 2, pp. 468-470)

20. Magdalen Accepts the Invitation

On the eve of the day appointed for the instruction, Magdalen with Martha and Anna Cleophas started from Magdalum to join the holy women at Damna, Magdalen rode on an ass, for she was not accustomed to walking. She was dressed elegantly, though not to such excess nor so extravagantly as at a later period when she was converted for the second time. She took a private apartment in the inn and spoke only with Dina and the Suphanite, who visited her by turns. I saw them together, an affable and well-bred confidence marking their intercourse. There was, however, on the part of the converted sinners, a shade of embarrassment similar to what might be experienced on a military officer's meeting a former comrade who had become a priest. This feeling soon gave way to tears and womanly expressions of mutual sympathy, and they went together to the inn at the foot of the mountain. The other holy women did not go to the instruction, in order not to annoy Magdalen by their presence. They had come to Damna with the intention of prevailing upon Jesus to remain there and not go to Capharnaum where Pharisees from various localities were again assembled. They, the Pharisees, had taken up their abode together, determined to make Capharnaum their headquarters for awhile, since it was the central point of all Jesus' journeyings. The young Pharisee from Samaria who was present the last time was not among this set; another had taken his place. At Nazareth also and in other places the Pharisees had formed similar unions against Jesus.

(Vol. 2, pp. 470-471)

---

21. The Mount of Instruction near Gabara

Magdalen and her companions reached the mountain in good time, and found crowds of people already encamped around it. The sick of all kinds were, according to the nature of their maladies, ranged together in different places under light canopies and arbors. High upon the mountain were the disciples, kindly ranging the people in order and rendering them every assistance. Around the teacher's chair was a low, semicircular wall, and over it an awning. The audience had here and there similar awnings erected. At a short distance from the teacher's chair, Magdalen and the other women had found a comfortable seat upon a little eminence.   (Vol. 2, p. 471)

---

22. Magdalen's First Conversion

Magdalen had taken her seat among the other women with the self-confident air of a lady of the world, but her manner was assumed. She was inwardly confused and a prey to interior struggle. At first she gazed around upon the crowd, but when Jesus appeared and began to speak, her eyes and soul were riveted upon Him alone. His exhortations to penance, His lively pictures of vice, His threats of chastisement, affected her powerfully, and unable to suppress her emotions, she trembled and wept beneath her veil. When Jesus, Himself shedding tears full of loving compassion, cried out for sinners to come to Him, many of His hearers were transported with emotion. There was a movement in the circle and the crowd pressed around Him. Magdalen also, and following her example the other women likewise, took a step nearer. But when Jesus exclaimed: "Ah! If even *one* soul would come to Me!" Magdalen was so moved that she wanted to fly to Him at once. She stepped forward; but her companions, fearing some disturbance, held her back, whispering: "Wait! Wait!" This movement of Magdalen attracted scarcely any notice among the bystanders, since the attention of all was riveted upon Jesus' words. Jesus, aware of Magdalen's agitation, uttered words of consolation meant only for her. He said: "If even one germ of penance, of contrition, of love, of

faith, of hope has, in consequence of My words, fallen upon
some poor, erring heart, it will bear fruit, it will be set
down in favor of that poor sinner, it will live and increase.
I Myself shall nourish it, shall cultivate it, shall present it
to My Father." These words consoled Magdalen while they
pierced her inmost soul, and she stepped back again
among her companions.   (Vol. 2, pp. 474-475)

23. Magdalen Witnesses Cures and Exorcisms

*It being late in the day, Jesus prays and dismisses
the multitude with His blessing. He and His
disciples begin their descent of the mountain and
are invited to dine at the home of Simon Zabulon,
the chief of the synagogue in Gabara.*

Magdalen and her companions followed Jesus. The former went among the people and took her place near the
sick women, as if to render them assistance. She was very
much impressed, and the misery that she witnessed
moved her still more. Jesus turned first to the men, among
whom for a long time He healed diseases of all kinds. The
hymns of thanksgiving from the cured and their attendants as they moved away, rang on the breeze. When He
approached the sick females, the crowd that pressed
around Him and the need that He and His disciples had
of space forced Magdalen and the holy women to fall back
a little. Nevertheless, Magdalen sought by every opportunity, by every break in the crowd, to draw near to Him, but
Jesus constantly turned away from her.

He healed some women afflicted with a flow of blood.
But how express the feelings of Magdalen, so delicate, so
effeminate, whose eyes were quite unused to the sight of
human suffering! What memories, what gratitude swelled
the heart of Mary Suphan when six women, bound three

and three, were forcibly led to Jesus by strong servant maids who dragged them along with cords, or long linen bands! They were possessed in the most frightful manner by unclean spirits, and they were the first possessed women that I saw brought publicly to Jesus. Some were from beyond the Lake of Genesareth, some from Samaria, and among them were several pagans. They had been bound together only upon reaching this place. Ordinarily they were perfectly quiet and gentle; they offered no violence to one another. But anon, they became quite furious, screaming and hurling themselves here and there. Their custodians bound them and kept them at a distance during Jesus' discourse, and now when all was nearly over, they brought them forward. As the afflicted creatures drew near to Jesus and the disciples, they began to offer vehement resistance. Satan was tormenting them horribly. They uttered the most awful cries and fell into violent contortions. Jesus turned toward them and commanded them to be silent, to be at peace. They instantly stood still and motionless; then He went up to them, ordered them to be unbound, commanded them to kneel down, prayed, and laid His hands upon them. Under the touch of His hand they sank into a few moments' unconsciousness, during which the wicked spirits went out of them in the form of a dark vapor. Then their attendants lifted them up, and veiled and in tears, they stood before Jesus, inclining low and giving thanks. He warned them to amend their lives, to purify themselves and do penance, lest their misfortune might come upon them more frightfully than before.

(Vol. 2, pp. 476-477)

---

24. Magdalen's First Anointing of Jesus

It was dusk before Jesus and the disciples, preceded

and followed by crowds of people, started at last down the mountain for Gabara. Magdalen, obeying only her impulse without regard to appearances, followed close after Jesus in the crowd of disciples, and her four companions, unwilling to separate from her, did the same. She tried to keep as close to Jesus as she possibly could, though such conduct was quite unusual in females. Some of the disciples called Jesus' attention to the fact, remarking at the same time what I have just observed. But Jesus, turning around to them, replied: "Let them alone! It is not your affair!" And so He entered the city. When He reached the hall in which Simon Zabulon had prepared the feast, He found the forecourt filled with the sick and the poor who had crowded thither on His approach, and who were loudly calling upon Him for help. Jesus at once turned to them, exhorting, consoling, and healing them. Meanwhile Simon Zabulon, with some other Pharisees, made his appearance. He begged Jesus to come in to the feast, for they were awaiting Him. "Thou hast," he continued, "already done enough for today. Let these people wait till another time, and let the poor go off at once." But Jesus replied: "These are My guests. I have invited them, and I must first see to their entertainment. When thou didst invite Me to thy feast, thou didst invite them also. I shall not go into thy feast until they are helped, and then even I will go in only with them." Then the Pharisees had to go and prepare tables around the court for the cured and the poor. Jesus cured all, and the disciples led those that wished to remain to the tables prepared for them, and lamps were lighted in the court.

Magdalen and the women had followed Jesus hither. They stood in one of the halls of the court adjoining the entertainment hall. Jesus, followed by some of the disciples, went to the table in the latter and from its sumptuous dishes sent various meats to the tables of the poor.

The disciples were the bearers of these gifts; they likewise served and ate with the poor. Jesus continued His instructions during the entertainment. The Pharisees were in animated discussion with Him when Magdalen, who with her companions had approached the entrance, all of a sudden darted into the hall. Inclining humbly, her head veiled, in her hand a little white flask closed with a tiny bunch of aromatic herbs instead of a stopper, she glided quickly into the center of the apartment, went behind Jesus, and poured the contents of her little flask over His head. Then catching up the long end of her veil, she folded it, and with both hands passed it lightly once over Jesus' head, as if wishing to smooth His hair and to arrest the overflow of the ointment. The whole affair occupied but a few instants, and after it Magdalen retired some steps. The discussion carried on so hotly at the moment suddenly ceased. A hush fell upon the company, and they gazed upon Jesus and the woman. The air was redolent with the fragrance of the ointment. Jesus was silent. Some of the guests put their heads together, glanced indignantly at Magdalen, and exchanged whispers. Simon Zabulon especially appeared scandalized. At last Jesus said to him: "Simon, I know well of what thou art thinking! Thou thinkest it improper that I should allow this woman to anoint My head. Thou art thinking that she is a sinner, but thou art wrong. She, out of love, has fulfilled what thou didst leave undone. Thou hast not shown Me the honor due to guests." Then He turned to Magdalen, who was still standing there, and said: "Go in peace! Much has been forgiven thee." At these words Magdalen rejoined her companions, and they left the house together. Then Jesus spoke of her to the guests. He called her a good woman full of compassion. He censured the criticizing of others, public accusations, and remarks upon the exterior fault of others while the speakers often hid in their own hearts much greater, though secret evils. Jesus continued speaking and teaching for a considerable time, and then returned with His followers to the inn. . . .

Magdalen's dress was white, embroidered with large red flowers and tiny green leaves. The sleeves were wide, gathered in and fastened by bracelets. The robe was cut wide and hung loose in the back. It was open in front to just above the knee, where it was caught by straps, or cords. The bodice, both back and front, was ornamented with cords and jewels. It passed over the shoulders like a scapular and was fastened at the sides; under it was another colored tunic. The veil that she usually wound about her neck she had, on entering the banquet hall, opened wide and thrown over her whole person. Magdalen was taller than all the other women, robust, but yet graceful. She had very beautiful, tapering fingers, a small, delicate foot, a wealth of beautiful long hair, and there was something imposing in all her movements. . . .

Magdalen was deeply touched and impressed by all she had seen and heard. She was interiorly vanquished. And because she was possessed of a certain impetuous spirit of self-sacrifice, a certain greatness of soul, she longed to do something to honor Jesus and to testify to Him her emotion. She had noticed with chagrin that neither before nor during the meal had He, the most wonderful, the holiest of teachers, He, the most compassionate, the most miraculous Helper of mankind, received from these Pharisees any mark of honor, any of those polite attentions usually extended to guests, and therefore she felt herself impelled to do what she had done. The words of Jesus, "If even one would be moved to come to Me!" still lingered in her memory. The little flask, which was about a hand in height, she generally carried with her, as do the grand ladies of our own day.   (Vol. 2, pp. 477-480)

_____

25. Magdalen Falls Back into Sin

When Magdalen returned to the inn with her companions, Martha took her to another about an hour distant
and near the baths of Bethulia. There she found Mary
and the holy women awaiting her coming. Mary conversed with her. Magdalen gave an account of Jesus'
discourse, while the two other women related the circumstances of Magdalen's anointing and Jesus' words to her.
All insisted on Magdalen's remaining and going back
with them, at least for awhile, to Bethania. But she
replied that she must return to Magdalum to make some
arrangements in her household, a resolution very distasteful to her pious friends. She could not, however,
cease talking of the impressions she had received and of
the majesty, force, sweetness, and miracles of Jesus. She
felt that she must follow Him, that her own life was an
unworthy one, and that she ought to join her sister and
friends. She became very thoughtful, she wept from time
to time, and her heart grew lighter. Nevertheless, she
could not be induced to remain, so she returned to Magdalum with her maid. Martha accompanied her a part of
the way, and then joined the holy women who were going
back to Capharnaum.

Magdalen was soon again in her old track. She received
the visits of men who spoke in the usual disparaging way
of Jesus. His journeys, His doctrine, and of all who followed Him. They ridiculed what they heard of Magdalen's
visit to Gabara, and looked upon it as a very unlikely
story. As for the rest, they declared that they found Magdalen more beautiful and charming than ever. It was by
such speeches that Magdalen allowed herself to be infatu-
ated and her good impressions dissipated. She soon sank
deeper than before, and her relapse into sin gave the devil

greater power over her. He attacked her more vigorously when he saw that he might possibly lose her. She became possessed, and often fell into cramps and convulsions.

(Vol. 2, pp. 480-481)

26. The Relationship between Sin and Illness

From Gabara, Jesus and His disciples travel to Capharnaum, where He performs many miraculous cures and exorcisms. The Pharisees of this city plan to have Jesus arrested, but His followers are too numerous. He teaches in the synagogue, where He expels a demon from a man raging through the crowd.

Next morning, Jesus again taught unmolested in the synagogue. The Pharisees had said to one another: "We can do nothing with Him now; His adherents are too numerous. We shall contradict Him now and then, we shall report all at Jerusalem and wait till He goes up to the Temple for the Pasch." The streets were again filled with the sick. Some had come before the Sabbath, and some till now had not believed, but on the report of the possessed man's cure, they had themselves transported thither from all quarters of the city. Many of them had been there before, but had not been cured. They were weak, tepid, slothful souls, more difficult to convert than great sinners of more ardent nature. Magdalen was converted only after many struggles and relapses, but her last efforts were generous and final. Dina the Samaritan turned at once from her evil ways, and the Suphanite, after sighing long for grace, was suddenly converted. All the great female sinners were very quickly and powerfully converted, as was also the sturdy Paul, to whom conversion came like a flash of lightning. Judas, on the contrary, was always vacillating, and at last fell into the abyss. It was the same with the great and most violent maladies which I saw Jesus, in His wisdom, cure at once. They that were afflicted with them, like the possessed, had no will whatever to remain in the state in which they were, or again, self-will was entirely overcome by the violence of the malady. But as to those that were less grievously affected, whose sufferings only opposed an obstacle to their sinning with more facility, and whose conversion was insincere, I saw that Jesus often sent them away with an admonition to reform their lives; or that He only alleviated without curing their bodily ills, that through their pressure the soul might be cured. Jesus could have cured all that came to Him, and that instantaneously, but He did so only for those that believed and did penance, and He frequently warned them against a relapse. Even those that were only slightly sick He sometimes cured at once, if such would prove beneficial to their soul. He was not come to cure the body that it might the more readily sin, but He cured the body in order to deliver and save the soul. In every malady, in every species of bodily infirmity, I see a special design of God. Sickness is the sign of some sin. It may be his own or another's, a sin of which he may be conscious or not, that the sufferer has to expiate, or it may be a trial expressly prepared for him, which by patience and submission to God's will he may change into capital that will yield a rich return. Properly speaking, no one suffers innocently, for who is innocent, since the Son of God had to take upon Himself the sins of the world that they might be blotted out? To follow Him, we are all obliged to bear our cross after Him.   (Vol. 3. pp. 7-8).

27. The Pharisees Confront Jesus In the Synagogue of Capharnaum

That evening when Jesus was teaching again in the synagogue, the Pharisees . . . began to dispute with Him on the subject of His forgiving sins. They reproached Him with the fact of His having in Gabara said to Mary Magdalen that her sins were forgiven her, and they asked how He knew that. How could He do that? Such talk was blasphemy! Jesus silenced them. Then they tried to provoke Him to say that He was not a man, that He was God. But Jesus again confounded them in their words. This scene took place in the forecourt of the synagogue. At last the Pharisees raised a great cry and tumult. But Jesus slipped from their hands and into the crowd, so that they could not tell where He had gone.   (Vol. 3, pp. 10-11)

---

28. Jesus Cures Two Scribes of Their Leprosy

After Jesus leaves the synagogue, He makes His way to His Blessed Mother's house. From thence He and His disciples travel to Mageddo, where they meet many of the disciples of John the Baptist. John has sent them in the hope that they will follow Jesus, but they return to John still unconvinced. Jesus and His disciples travel slowly back to Capharnaum, stopping at many places to teach or heal all who come into their path.

Jesus . . . passed by the estate of the Centurion Zorobabel, as He and His disciples were hurrying along, for the Sabbath had already begun. In his charity, Zorobabel had permitted two young Scribes of about twenty-five years, who on account of their dissolute life had been stricken with leprosy, to take up their abode in his garden. They were perfectly loathsome to look upon, and in their misery subjected to the greatest contempt. The red mantles that enveloped them hid the ulcers with which they were covered. They had once formed a part of Magdalen's gay coterie at Magdalum, had afterward carried on their excesses in other places, and fell at last into the extreme misery in which they now were. At Jesus' recent visit to these parts, they were ashamed to present themselves before Him, but now, convinced by the news of His miracles and great mercy, they had allowed themselves to be dragged to a place near the road by which He would pass and where they could cry to Him for help. Jesus would not pause. He hurried on, but told two of Zorobabel's servants, who came running after Him, pleading for the unfortunate creatures, to bring them to the synagogue in Capharnaum. When the people were assembled, they (the servants) were to conduct the lepers to the gallery, one story high, that had been built adjoining the synagogue, and from which the teaching going on inside could be heard by those from without. There they should pray and excite themselves to contrition until He should call them. The servants immediately hastened back, and took the poor men by a shortcut through the flowery ravine to Capharnaum. They dragged them, though not without difficulty, up the outside steps to the gallery where, leaning in at the windows of the synagogue, they could, apart from the throng and in the open air, listen to the teachings of Jesus and with penitent hearts await their Saviour's call. (Vol. 3, pp. 31-32)

---

29. Magdalen Suffers from Demonic Possession

After Jesus is finished teaching in the synagogue, He calls the two scribes down from the gallery, and, exhorting them to continence and penance, He heals them.

He raises the daughter of Jairus from the dead.
In Corozain He blesses Peter, Andrew, James and
John, giving them the graces needed to bless water for
Baptism. Jesus calms the storm on the Sea of Galilee.
Foreseeing his own death, John the Baptist again tells
his disciples to leave him and follow Jesus. In Corozain
there are enormous crowds gathering to hear Jesus
and be healed by Him. The disciples, to supply food
for the multitude, try all night to catch fish. Returning
unsuccessful, they are told by Jesus to cast their nets
again, whereupon they miraculously catch more in
this one try than they had ever caught before in
months together. Jesus travels to Magdala, where
He delivers many from demonic possession.

Jesus next visited His Mother, with whom were then
stopping Susanna Alpheus, Mary, the daughter of
Cleophas of Nazareth, Susanna of Jerusalem, Dina the
Samaritan, and Martha. Jesus told them that He was
going away the next morning. Martha was very sad on
account of Magdalen's relapse into sin and the state of
demoniacal possession in which she then was. She asked
Jesus whether she should go to her, but He told her to
wait awhile. Magdalen was now often like one beside
herself. She yielded to fits of anger and pride, struck all
that came in her way, tormented her maids, and was
always arrayed in the most wanton attire. I saw her
striking the man that lived as master in her house, and
I beheld him returning her blows with ill-treatment. At
times she fell into frightful sadness; she wept and
lamented. She ran about the house seeking for Jesus and
crying out: "Where is the Teacher? Where is He? He has
abandoned me!" and then fell into convulsions like
epileptic fits.   (Vol. 3, p. 94)

30. Mary the Suphanite Confounded With Mary Magdalen

Martha and Susanna had visited their inns on the way through Galilee to Samaria, for they exercised a kind of general superintendence, the other women seeing to those established in their own respective districts. They went together to the several inns, taking with them asses laden with all kinds of household necessaries. Once, when Mary the Suphanite accompanied them, the report spread among the people that Mary Magdalen now went around with the women who provided for the needs of the Prophet of Nazareth and His party. The Suphanite was in figure very like Magdalen, and neither of them was very well-known on this side of the Jordan. Besides being called Mary and the ill repute her past life had gained for her, the Suphanite also had anointed Jesus at a feast given by one of the Pharisees. She was consequently, even at this early date, confounded with Magdalen, a mistake that only increased with time among those not well acquainted with the Community.   (Vol. 3, pp. 94-95)

31. External Appearance of Magdalen, Dina And the Blessed Virgin

Magdalen was taller and more beautiful than the other women. Dina, however, was much more active and dexterous, very cheerful, ever ready to oblige, like a lively, affectionate girl, and she was moreover very humble. But the Blessed Virgin surpassed them all in her marvelous beauty. Although in external loveliness she may have had her equal, and may have even been excelled by Magdalen in certain striking features, yet she far outshone them all in her indescribable air of simplicity, modesty, earnestness, sweetness, and gentleness. She was so very pure, so free from all earthly impressions that in her one saw only the reflex image of God in His creature. No one's bearing resembled hers, except that of her Son. Her countenance surpassed that of all women in its unspeakable purity, innocence, gravity, wisdom, peace, and sweet, devout loveliness. Her whole appearance was noble, and yet she was like a simple, innocent child. She was very grave, very quiet, and often pensive, but never did her sadness destroy the beauty of her countenance, for her tears flowed softly down her placid face.   (Vol. 2, pp. 480-481)

---

32. Martha Persuades Magdalen to See Jesus Again

The crowds being too great and excited, Jesus and His disciples leave Capharnaum. Jesus lays His hands on His Apostles and blesses His disciples, telling them to teach and heal in His name. Jesus and some of His disciples meet the holy women at the inn at Dothain.

About an hour to the south of the inn at Dothain lay the little town of Azanoth. It was built on an eminence upon which was a teacher's chair and, in earlier times, it had often been the scene of the Prophet's preaching. Through the activity of the disciples, the report had been spread throughout the whole region that Jesus was about to deliver a great instruction in that place, and in consequence of this report, multitudes were gathered there from all Galilee. Martha, attended by her maid, had journeyed to Magdalen, in the hope of inducing her to be present at the instruction, but she was received very haughtily by her sister, with whom things had come to the worst. She was, on Martha's arrival, engaged at her toilet, and sent word that she could not speak to her then.

Martha awaited her sister's appearance with unspeakable patience, occupying herself meanwhile in prayer. At last the unhappy Magdalen presented herself, her manner haughty, excited, and defiant. She was ashamed of Martha's simple attire. She feared that some of her guests might see her; consequently, she requested her to go away as soon as possible. But Martha, begging to be allowed to rest in some corner of the house, she and her maid were conducted to a room in one of the side buildings where, either through design or forgetfulness, they were allowed to remain without food or drink. It was then afternoon. Meanwhile, Magdalen adorned herself for the banquet, at which she was seated on a richly decorated chair, while Martha and her maid were in prayer. After the revelry, Magdalen went at last to Martha, taking with her something on a little blue-edged plate and something to drink. She addressed Martha angrily and disdainfully, her whole demeanor expressive of pride, insolence, uneasiness and interior agitation. Martha, full of humility and affection, invited Magdalen to go with her once more to the great instruction Jesus was going to deliver in the neighborhood. All Magdalen's female friends, Martha urged, those whom she had lately met, would be there and very glad to see her. She herself (Magdalen) had already testified to the esteem in which she held Jesus, and she should now gratify Lazarus and herself (Martha) by going once more to hear Him preach. She would not soon again have the opportunity of hearing the wonderful Prophet and at the same time of seeing all her friends in her own neighborhood. She had shown by her anointing of Jesus at the banquet at Gabara that she knew how to honor greatness and majesty. She should now again salute Him whom she had once so nobly and fearlessly honored in public, etc., etc. It would be impossible to say how lovingly Martha spoke to her erring sister, or how patiently she endured her shamefully contemptuous manner. At last Magdalen replied: "I shall go, but not with you! You can go on ahead, for I will not be seen with one so miserably clothed. I shall dress according to my position, and I shall go with my own friends." At these words, the two sisters separated, for it was very late.   (Vol. 3, pp. 122-123)

---

33. Magdalen's Extravagant Attire

Next morning Magdalen sent for Martha to come to her room while she was making her toilet. Martha went, patient as usual and secretly praying that Magdalen might go with her and be converted. Magdalen, clothed in a fine woolen garment, was sitting on a low stool, while two of her maids were busily engaged washing her feet and arms and perfuming them with fragrant water. Her hair was divided into three parts above the ears and at the back of the head, after which it was combed, brushed, oiled, and braided. Over her fine woolen undergarment was put a green robe embroidered with large yellow flowers, and over that again a mantle with folds. Her head-dress was a kind of crimped cap that rose high on the forehead. Both her hair and her cap were interwoven with numberless pearls, and in her ears were long pendants. Her sleeves were wide above the elbow, but narrow below and fastened with broad, glittering bracelets. Her robe was plaited. Her under-bodice was open on the breast and laced with shining cords. During the toilet, Magdalen held in her hand a round, polished mirror. She wore an ornament on her breast. It was covered with gold, and encrusted with cut stones and pearls. Over the narrow-sleeved underdress she wore an upper one with a long flowing train and short, wide sleeves. It was made of changeable violet silk, and embroidered with large flow-

ers, some in gold, others in different colors. The braids of
her hair were ornamented with roses made of raw silk,
and strings of pearls, interwoven with some kind of stiff
transparent stuff that stood out in points. Very little of
the hair could be seen through its load of ornamentation.
It was rolled high around the face. Over this headdress,
Magdalen wore a rich hood of fine, transparent material.
It fell on the high headdress in front, shaded the cheeks,
and hung low on the shoulders behind.(Vol. 3, pp. 123-
124)

34. Magdalen and Her Companions Set Out to Attend Jesus' Instruction

Martha took leave of her sister, and went to the inn
near Damna, in order to tell Mary and the holy women the
success she had had in her efforts to persuade Magdalen
to be present at the instruction about to be given in Azanoth. With the Blessed Virgin, about a dozen women had to
come to Damna, among them Anna Cleophas, Susanna of
Jerusalem, Veronica, Johanna Chusa, Mary Marcus, Dina,
Maroni, and the Suphanite.

Jesus, accompanied by six Apostles and a number of
the disciples, started from the inn at Dothain for Azanoth.
On the way, He met the holy women coming from Damna.
Lazarus was among Jesus' companions on this occasion.

After Martha's departure, Magdalen was very much
tormented by the devil, who wanted to prevent her going
to Jesus' instruction. She would have followed his sug-
gestions, were it not for some of her guests, who had
agreed to go with her to Azanoth, to witness what they
called a great show. Magdalen and her frivolous, sinful
companions rode on asses to the inn of the holy women
near the Baths of Bethulia. Magdalen's splendid seat,

along with cushions and rugs for the others, followed, packed on asses. (Vol. 3, pp. 124-125)

---

35. Magdalen's Second Conversion

Next morning Magdalen, again arrayed in her most wanton attire and surrounded by her companions, made her appearance at the place of instruction, which was about an hour from the inn at which she was stopping. With noise and bustle, loud talk and bold staring about, they took their places under an open tent in front of the holy women. There were some men of their own stamp in their party. They sat upon cushions and rugs and upholstered chairs, all in full view, Magdalen in front. Their coming gave rise to general whispering and murmurs of disapprobation, for they were even more detested and despised in these quarters than in Gabara. The Pharisees especially, who knew of her first remarkable conversion at Gabara and of her subsequent relapse into her former disorders, were scandalized and expressed their indignation at her daring to appear in such an assembly.

Jesus, after healing many sick, began His long and severe discourse. The details of His sermon, I cannot now recall, but I know that He cried woe upon Capharnaum, Bethsaida, and Corozain. He said also that the Queen of Saba had come from the South to hear the wisdom of Solomon, but here was One greater than Solomon. And lo, the wonder! Children that had never yet spoken, babes in their mother's arms, cried out from time to time during the instruction: "Jesus of Nazareth! Holiest of Prophets! Son of David! Son of God!" Which words caused many of the hearers, and among them Magdalen, to tremble with fear. Making allusion to Magdalen, Jesus said that when the devil has been driven out and the house has been swept, he returns with six other demons, and rages worse than before. These words terrified Magdalen. After Jesus had in this way touched the hearts of many, He turned successively to all sides and commanded the demon to go out of all that sighed for deliverance from this thralldom, but that those who wished to remain bound to the devil should depart and take him along with them. At this command, the possessed cried out from all parts of the circle: "Jesus, Thou Son of God!"—and here and there people sank to the ground unconscious.

Magdalen also, from her splendid seat upon which she had attracted all eyes, fell in violent convulsions. Her companions in sin applied perfumes as restoratives, and wanted to carry her away. Desiring to remain under the empire of the evil one, they were themselves glad to profit by the opportunity to retire from the scene. But just then some person near her cried out: "Stop, Master! Stop! This woman is dying." Jesus interrupted His discourse to reply: "Place her on her chair! The death she is now dying is a good death, and one that will vivify her!" After some time another word of Jesus pierced her to the heart, and she again fell into convulsions, during which dark forms escaped from her. A crowd gathered round her in alarm, while her own immediate party tried once again to bring her to herself. She was soon able to resume her seat on her beautiful chair, and then she tried to look as if she had suffered only an ordinary fainting spell. She had now become the object of general attention, especially as many other possessed back in the crowd had, like her, fallen in convulsions, and afterward rose up freed from the evil one. But when for the third time Magdalen fell down in violent convulsions, the excitement increased, and Martha hurried forward to her. When she recovered consciousness, she acted like one bereft of her senses. She wept passionately, and wanted to go to where the holy women were sitting. The frivolous companions with whom she had come hither held her back forcibly, declaring that she should not play the fool, and they at last succeeded in getting her down the mountain. Lazarus, Martha, and others who had followed her, now went forward and led her to the inn of the holy women. The crowd of worldlings who had accompanied Magdalen had already made their way off.

Before going down to His inn, Jesus healed many blind and sick. Later on, He taught again in the school, and Magdalen was present. She was not yet quite cured, but profoundly impressed, and no longer so wantonly arrayed. She had laid aside her superfluous finery, some of which was made of a fine scalloped material like pointed lace, and so perishable that it could be worn only once. She was now veiled. Jesus in His instruction appeared again to speak for her special benefit and, when He fixed upon her His penetrating glance, she fell once more into unconsciousness and another evil spirit went out of her. Her maids bore her from the synagogue to where she was received by Martha and Mary, who took her back to the inn. She was now like one distracted. She cried and wept. She ran through the public streets saying to all she met that she was a wicked creature, a sinner, the refuse of humanity. The holy women had the greatest trouble to quiet her. She tore her garments, disarranged her hair, and hid her face in the folds of her veil. When Jesus returned to His inn with the disciples and some of the Pharisees, and while they were taking some refreshments standing, Magdalen escaped from the holy women, ran with streaming hair and uttering loud lamentations, made her way through the crowd, cast herself at Jesus' feet, weeping and moaning, and asked if she might still hope for salvation. The Pharisees and disciples, scandalized at the sight, said to Jesus that He should no longer suffer this reprobate woman to create disturbance every-

where, that He should send her away once and for all. But
Jesus replied: "Permit her to weep and lament! Ye know
not what is passing in her"—and He turned to her with
words of consolation. He told her to repent from her heart,
to believe and to hope, for that she should soon find peace.
Then He bade her depart with confidence. Martha, who
had followed with her maids, took her again to the inn.
Magdalen did nothing but wring her hands and lament.
She was not yet quite freed from the power of the evil one,
who tortured and tormented her with the most frightful
remorse and despair. There was no rest for her—she
thought herself forever lost.

To escape the great crowd that had gathered here,
Jesus went that night with His disciples into the neighborhood of Damna, where there was an inn, as well as a
lovely eminence upon which stood a chair for teaching.
Next morning when the holy women came thither accompanied by Magdalen, they found Jesus already encompassed by people seeking His aid. When His departure
became known, the crowds awaiting Him at Azanoth, as
well as new visitors, came streaming to Damna, and fresh
bands continued to arrive during the whole instruction.

Magdalen, crushed and miserable, now sat among the
holy women. Jesus inveighed severely against the sin of
impurity, and said that it was that vice that had called
down fire upon Sodom and Gomorrha. But He spoke of the
mercy of God also and of the present time of pardon,
almost conjuring His hearers to accept the grace offered
them. Thrice during this discourse did Jesus rest His
glance upon Magdalen, and each time I saw her sinking
down and dark vapors issuing from her. The third time,
the holy women carried her away. She was pale, weak,
annihilated as it were, and scarcely recognizable. Her
tears flowed incessantly. She was completely transformed,
and passionately sighed to confess her sins to Jesus and

receive pardon. The instruction over, Jesus went to a retired place, whither Mary herself and Martha led Magdalen to Him. She fell on her face weeping at His feet, her hair flowing loosely around her. Jesus comforted her. When Mary and Martha had withdrawn, she cried for pardon, confessed her numerous transgressions, and asked over and over: "Lord, is there still salvation for me?" Jesus forgave her sins, and she implored Him to save her from another relapse. He promised to do so, gave her His blessing, and spoke to her of the virtue of purity, also of His Mother, who was pure without stain. He praised Mary highly in terms I had never before heard from His lips, and commanded Magdalen to unite herself closely to her and to seek from her advice and consolation. When Jesus and Magdalen rejoined the holy women, Jesus said to them: "She has been a great sinner, but for all future time, she will be the model of penitents."

Magdalen, through her passionate emotion, her grief and her tears, was no longer like a human being, but like a shadow tottering from weakness. She was, however, calm, though still weeping silent tears that exhausted her. The holy women comforted her with many marks of affection, while she in turn craved pardon of each. As they had to set out for Naim and Magdalen was too weak to accompany them, Martha, Anna Cleophas, and Mary the Suphanite went with her to Damna, in order to rest that night and follow the others next morning. The holy women went through Cana to Naim.

Upon her request, Lazarus went to Magdalum in order to take charge of her property, and dissolve the ties she had there formed. She owned near Azanoth and in the surrounding country fields and vineyards which Lazarus, on account of her extravagance, had previously sequestered.   (Vol. 3, pp. 125-130)

36. News of Magdalen's Conversion Spreads

Jesus and His disciples make their way to Nazareth,
where He is well received; but the Pharisees,
on learning that He does not intend to stay,
become insolent. He cures many here and
settles many disputes among neighbors.

When Jesus was leaving the synagogue, three women presented themselves before Him, requesting a private interview. When He withdrew with them from the crowd, they cast themselves on their knees before Him, and made their laments over their husbands, whom they begged Jesus to help. Their husbands, they said, were tormented by evil spirits, by whom they themselves were sometimes attacked. They had heard, they said, that He had helped Magdalen, and they hoped that He would likewise have pity on them. Jesus promised to visit their homes. He went first, however, with His disciples to the house of a certain Simeon, a simple-hearted man belonging to the married Essenians. He was of middle age and the son of a Pharisee of Dabereth on Thabor. Jesus and the disciples partook, in this house, of refreshments standing. Simeon was desirous of bestowing all his goods upon the Community, and he spoke with Jesus to that effect.

On leaving Simeon's, Jesus went as He had promised to the homes of the women, and had an interview with them and their husbands. Affairs were not just as the wives had stated, for they had thrown upon their husbands the blame of which they were themselves deserving. Jesus exhorted both parties to live in harmony, to pray, to fast, and to give alms. After the Sabbath these infirm women followed Jesus to a mountain a little to the north of Thabor where He was going to deliver a discourse. He did not remain long there. He went southward toward Kisloth, which city the holy women passed on their road to Naim, Magdalen also, when journeying with her party. On the way Jesus again instructed the Apostles upon what was in store for them. He told them how they should behave when they arrived in Judea, where they would not be so well received. He gave them new directions as to their conduct, also for the imposition of hands and the driving out of the demon, and as an additional source of strength and increase of grace, He again conferred upon them His benediction.

(Vol. 3, pp. 132-133)

It was still dawn when Jesus left the house and went out on the road where were awaiting Him about five men and women. From a retired spot, a little off from the road, they cried to Him for assistance. Jesus stepped to them, and they cast themselves at His feet. One of the women addressed Him: "Lord, we are from Tiberias, and until now we have hesitated to implore Thy help. The Pharisees told us that Thou art hard and pitiless toward sinners. But we have heard of Thy merciful compassion to Magdalen, whom Thou didst free from her miseries, and whose sins Thou didst also forgive. All this gave us courage, and we have followed Thee thither. Lord, have mercy on us! Thou canst heal us and purify us. Thou canst likewise forgive us our sins." The men and women were standing apart from one another. They were afflicted with leprosy and other maladies. One woman was possessed by a wicked spirit who threw her into convulsions.

Jesus took them aside, one by one, to hear the particulars of their confession, inasmuch as the detailed account would serve to increase their sorrow and repentance. He did not exact this from all, unless it was necessary. He cured those of whom we are now speaking, and forgave them their sins. They melted into tears of gratitude, and begged Him to say what they should henceforth do. In reply, Jesus commanded them not to return to Tiberias, but to go to another place.   (Vol. 3, p. 138)

---

37. The Holy Women Care for the Inns

The holy women, Mary, Veronica, Susanna, Magdalen, and Mary the Suphanite, were now in Dothan near Samaria. They were stopping with Issachar, the sick husband, whom Jesus had lately healed. The holy women never went to the public inns. Martha, Dina, Johanna Chusa, Susanna Alpheus, Anna Cleophas, Mary Johanna Marcus, and Maroni went, two by two, to look after the inns and supply what was wanting. There were about twelve of these women.   (Vol. 3, p. 142)

---

38. Jesus Defends the Converted Holy Women

*Jesus sends the Apostles into hostile parts of
the country to preach penance. John the Baptist
is beheaded at the request of Herodias' daughter
Salome. Jesus, Peter and John journey to Antipatris,
where He cures a paralytic girl. The Pharisees jeer
and insult Him as He teaches in the synagogue
of that city, ascribing His miracles to sorcery.
Jesus, Peter and John travel to Bethoron.
They are much better received by the
Pharisees here, who invite them to a dinner.*

During the meal, the Pharisees addressed to Him all kinds of reproaches; among others, they alleged that He allowed women of bad repute to follow Him about. These men had heard of the conversion of Magdalen, of Mary Suphan, and of the Samaritan. Jesus replied: "If ye knew Me, ye would speak differently. I am come to have pity on sinners." He contrasted external ulcers, which carry off poisonous humors and are easily healed, with internal ones which, though full of loathsome matter, do not affect the appearance of the individual so afflicted. The Pharisees further alleged that His disciples had neglected to wash before the meal, which gave Jesus an opportunity for a timely and energetic protest against the hypocrisy and sanctimoniousness of the Pharisees themselves. When they spoke of the women of ill repute, Jesus related a parable. He asked which was the more praiseworthy, the debtor, who having a great debt, humbly implored indulgence until he could faithfully discharge it little by little; or another who, though deeply in debt, spent all he could lay his hands on in rioting and, far from thinking of paying what he owed, mocked at the conscientious debtor. Jesus related likewise the parables of the good shepherd and the vineyard, as He had done at Antipatris, but His hearers were indifferent; they did not seize the application.   (Vol. 3, pp. 159)

39. Magdalen Begins Her Life as a Penitent

From Bethoron, which was six hours distant from Jerusalem, Jesus went straight on to Bethania, stopping at no place on the way, excepting Athanot. Lazarus had already returned to Bethania from Magdalum, where he had put everything in order and engaged a steward for the castle and other property. To the man who had lived with Magdalen, he had assigned a dwelling situated on the heights near Ginnim and sufficient means for his support. The gift was gladly accepted.

As soon as she arrived in Bethania, Magdalen went straight to the dwelling of her deceased sister, Mary the Silent, by whom she had been very much beloved, and spent the whole night in tears. When Martha went to her in the morning, she found her weeping on the grave of her sister, her hair unbound and flowing around her.

The women of Jerusalem also had returned to their homes, all making the journey on foot. Magdalen, though exhausted by her malady and the shocks she had received, and wholly unaccustomed to such travelling, insisted upon walking like the others. Her feet bled more than once. The holy women who, since her conversion, showed her unspeakable affection, were often obliged to come to her assistance. She was pale and exhausted from weeping. She could not resist her desire to express her gratitude to Jesus, so she went over an hour's journey to meet Him, threw herself at His feet, and bedewed them with repentant and grateful tears. Jesus extended His hand to her, raised her, and addressed to her words of kindness. He spoke of her deceased sister, Mary the Silent. He said that she should tread in her footsteps and do penance as she had done, although she had never sinned. Magdalen then returned home with her maid by another way.

Magdalen occupied the little apartments of Mary the Silent's dwelling. She often sat in a very narrow little room that appeared to be formed in a tower. It was a retired corner intended for penitential exercises. She still wept freely. True, she was no longer actually sick, but from contrition and penance, she had become quite pale and reduced. She looked like one crushed by sorrow.

(Vol. 3, pp. 160, 188)

40. Jesus Frees the Prisoners at Tirzah

*From Bethoron Jesus travels to Hebron, where He visits
the tomb of the Patriarchs. Word of John the Baptist's
death spreads, and some of the disciples and holy women
journey to Machaerus to retrieve his body and head,
which they carry back to Hebron to be entombed. Jesus
cures the man paralyzed thirty-eight years at the Pool
of Bethsaida. He teaches in the Temple during the Feast
of Three Days. He and His disciples then journey to
Tirzah, where Jesus visits those imprisoned for debt.*

Jesus then pressed the head men among the magis-
trates and Pharisees to go with Him to the Roman superintendent of the prison, and offer to ransom the most
miserable and neglected of the inmates. This proposal was
made in the hearing of many; consequently, the Pharisees
could not refuse. When Jesus and His disciples turned off
toward the residence of the superintendent, a crowd followed, sounding Jesus' praises. The superintendent was a
much better man than the Pharisees, who maliciously ran
up the prisoners' debts so high that, for the release of some
of them, Jesus had to pay fourfold. But because He had not
the money around Him, He gave as a pledge a triangular
coin to which hung a parchment ticket, upon which He had
written some words authorizing the sum to be discharged
from Magdalen's property, which Lazarus was about to
sell. The entire proceeds were destined by Magdalen and
Lazarus for the benefit of the poor, for debtors, and the
relief of sinners. Magdalum was a more valuable estate
than that of Bethania. Each side of the triangular coin was
about three inches long, and in the center was an inscription indicating its value. To one end hung a jointed strip of
metal, like two or three links of a chain, and to this the
writing was fastened.   (Vol. 3, pp. 203-204)

---

41. Jesus Arrives at Lazarus' for the Paschal Solemnity

*After the prisoners are released, Jesus again travels
to Capharnaum, where the Pharisees are investigating
His cures. Word of Jesus' return has spread, and there
are massive crowds awaiting Him. All of the twelve
Apostles have returned from their teaching, along with
the disciples. They assist Jesus by healing, exorcising
and teaching throughout the multitude. Jesus feeds the
five thousand with five loaves and two fishes.
He walks on the water of the Sea of Galilee and teaches
at the Synagogue of Capharnaum on the Bread of Life.
From thence Jesus travels to mostly pagan cities,
where He is well-received. He feeds the four thousand
with seven loaves and seven fishes. He promises Peter the
Keys to His Kingdom. Jesus and His disciples make
their way toward Bethania and Jerusalem
to celebrate the Pasch at the home of Lazarus.*

About three hours from Bethania, but still in the
desert, stood a solitary shepherd hut whose occupants
depended for the most part on the charity of Lazarus. To
this abode, Magdalen with a single companion, Mary
Salome, a relative of Joseph, had come to meet Jesus. She
had prepared for Him some refreshments. On His
approach, she hurried out and embraced His feet. Jesus
rested here only a short time and then set out for
Lazarus' inn, one hour from Bethania. The two women
returned home by another way. Jesus found some of the
disciples whom He had sent on their mission already
returned and at the inn; others came later, and in Bethania all met again. Jesus did not go through Bethania, but
entered Lazarus' dwelling from the rear. On His arrival,
all hurried out into the court to meet Him. Lazarus
washed His feet, and then they passed up through the

gardens. The women saluted Jesus with their veils lowered. A very touching incident attended Jesus' arrival. The four lambs destined for the Paschal solemnity were brought in at the same moment that Jesus entered. They had been separated from the flock and turned into a little grassy park. The Blessed Virgin, who also was here, and Magdalen had twined little wreaths which were to be hung around their necks. Jesus' coming was just before the commencement of the Sabbath, and He celebrated it with the family in a hall. He was very grave. He read the lesson for the Sabbath, and gave an instruction upon it. During the evening meal, He spoke of the Paschal lamb and of His future Passion.   (Vol. 3, pp. 274-275)

42. Magdalen's Love for Jesus

On the Sabbath Jesus taught in Lazarus', and then all went to walk in the gardens. Jesus talked of His Passion and said in plain terms that He was the Christ. His words increased His hearers' reverence and admiration for Him, while Magdalen's love and contrition reached their height. She followed Jesus everywhere, sat at His feet, stood and waited for Him everywhere. She thought of Him alone, saw Him alone, knew only her Redeemer and her own sins. Jesus frequently addressed to her words of consolation. She was very greatly changed. Her countenance and bearing was still noble and distinguished, though her beauty was destroyed by her penance and tears. She sat almost always alone in her narrow penance chamber, and at times performed the lowest services for the poor and sick.

(Vol. 3, pp. 275-276)

43. Jesus Admonishes His Followers To Pray without Ceasing

I saw Jesus several times walking with the disciples and other friends on the Mount of Olives, while Mary, Magdalen, and other women promenaded at some distance. I saw the disciples snapping off ears from the ripe cornfields, and here and there eating fruits and berries. Jesus gave the disciples minute instructions on prayer, warned them against hypocrisy in it, and repeated to them many things that He had before said. He likewise admonished them ever to walk by uninterrupted prayer in the presence of God, His own and their Father.

(Vol. 3, p. 280)

---

44. Mercuria

After the Pasch, Jesus and His disciples travel toward the city of Tiberias, staying a few days here and there, teaching and healing along the way. Jesus is transfigured on Mount Thabor. He sends the Apostles and disciples, to teach in the surrounding area for thirty days before rejoining Him. During this time, He and a few followers sail to the island of Cyprus, where he converts many, both Jewish and pagan, and is met with respect everywhere He goes.

When Jesus had returned to the inn with the disciples, a pagan came to Him and begged Him to go with him to a certain garden a few steps distant, where a person in distress was waiting to implore His assistance. Jesus went with the disciples to the place indicated. There He saw standing between the walls on the road a pagan lady, who inclined low before Him. He ordered the disciples to fall back a little, and then questioned the woman as to what she wanted. She was a very remarkable person, perfectly destitute of instruction, quite sunk in paganism, and wholly given up to its abominable service. One glance from Jesus had cast her into disquiet, and roused in her the feeling that she was in error, but she was without simple faith, and had a very confused manner of accusing herself. She told Jesus that she had heard of His having helped Magdalen, as also the woman afflicted with the issue, of whom the latter had merely touched the hem of His garment. She begged Jesus to cure and instruct her, but then again, she said perhaps He could not cure her as she was not, like the woman with the issue, physically sick. She confessed that she was married and had three children, but that one, unknown to her husband, had been begotten in adultery. She had also intercourse with the Roman Commandant. When Jesus, on the preceding day, visited the last named, she had watched Him from a window and saw a halo of light around His head, which sight very powerfully impressed her. She at first thought that her emotion sprang from love for Jesus, and the idea caused her anguish so intense that she fell to the ground unconscious. When returned to herself, her whole life, her whole interior passed before her in so frightful a manner that she entirely lost her peace of mind. She then made inquiries about Jesus, and learned from some Jewish women of Magdalen's cure, also that of Enue of Caesarea-Philippi, the woman afflicted with the issue of blood. She now implored Jesus to heal her if He possibly could. Jesus told her that the faith of that afflicted woman was simple; that, in the firm belief that if she could touch only the seam of His garment she would be cured, she had approached Him stealthily and her faith had saved her.

The silly woman again asked Jesus how He could have known that Enue touched Him and that He healed her. She did not comprehend Jesus or His power, although she heartily longed for His assistance. Jesus rebuked her, commanded her to renounce her shameful life, and told her of God the Almighty and His Commandment: "Thou shalt not commit adultery." He placed before her all the abominations of the debauchery (against which her nature itself revolted) practiced in the impure service of her gods; and He met her with words so earnest and so full of mercy that she retired weeping and penetrated with sorrow. The lady's name was Mercuria. She was tall, and about twenty-five years old. She was enveloped in a white mantle, long and flowing in the back but rather shorter in front, which formed a cap around the head. Her other garments also were white, though with colored borders.   (Vol. 3, pp. 355-357)

----

45. The Work of the Holy Women

There are now about twelve holy women who travel about the country, two by two, looking after the inns or working and praying together.

Magdalen and the Suphanite were nothing like as beautiful as they used to be. They were pale and thin, and their eyes red from weeping. Martha was very energetic, and in business affairs very talkative. Johanna Chusa was a tall, pale, vigorous woman, grave in manner, but at the same time active. Veronica had in her deportment something very like St. Catherine; she was frank, resolute, and courageous. When the holy women were thus gathered together, they used to work industriously, sewing and preparing for the Community all sorts of things, which were distributed among their private inns, or laid away in the storerooms. From these latter the Apostles and disciples supplied their own needs, as well as those of the poor. When there was no special work of this kind to be done, the holy women spent their time in sewing for poor synagogues. They generally had with them their maid-servants, who preceded or followed them on their journeys, and carried the various materials, sometimes in leathern pouches, sometimes attached to their girdle under their mantle. These maids wore tightly fitting bodices and short tunics. When the holy women were to remain some time at any place, their maids returned and awaited their coming at some of the inns along the route. Veronica's maid was with her a long time. She was in her service even after Jesus' death.

(Vol. 3, pp. 434-435)

46. Lazarus

While in Cyprus, Jesus visits and teaches people from all walks of life, converting many, some of whom leave everything to follow Him back to Israel. When He arrives in Israel, He journeys to Thanac, where He cures a man who was His enemy, converting him. Jesus meets Lazarus at an inn outside Damna, where he has been attending to Magdalen's estate of Magdalum.

Lazarus and two disciples belonging to Jerusalem were awaiting Him. Indeed, Lazarus had already been eight days in those parts attending to the real estate in land and houses of the Magdalum property, for only the household goods and similar effects belonging to Magdalen had as yet been disposed of. Jesus embraced Lazarus, a favor He was accustomed to extend only to him and the elder Apostles and disciples; to the others, He merely extended His hands. . . .

Lazarus was very refined in his manners, his whole demeanor earnest, quiet, and marked by a dignified affability; he spoke little, and his bearing toward Jesus was full of loving devotedness. . . .

Jesus treated Lazarus with marked confidence. On this

occasion they walked alone together for a long time. Lazarus was a tall man, grave and gentle and very self-possessed in manner. Moderate in all things, even his familiar intercourse with others was stamped with a something that wore an air of distinction. His hair was black and he bore some resemblance to Joseph, though his features were sterner and more marked. Joseph's hair was yellow, and there was something uncommonly tender, gentle, and obliging in his whole deportment.

(Vol. 2, p. 46; Vol. 3, pp. 439-440)

---

47. Lazarus Falls Ill

From Damna, Jesus travels to His Blessed Mother's house near Capharnaum to visit her and the holy women. All of the Apostles and disciples rejoin Him in Capharnaum, each giving Him an account of their journeys. Jesus stays in this area for some time, teaching and curing those in need. From here Jesus and His disciples make their way down to Jericho, where they are met by great crowds of people, imploring His blessing. A chief publican of the city named Zacheus climbs a fig tree to get a better view of the Prophet.

Before Jesus' departure from Jericho, messengers from Bethania brought to the disciples the news of how earnestly Martha and Magdalen were longing for His coming, as Lazarus was very sick. Jesus, however, did not go to Bethania, but to a little village north of Jericho. Here too, a crowd had assembled, and numbers of sick, blind, and crippled were awaiting His arrival. Two blind men, each with two guides, were sitting by the roadside, and when Jesus passed by, they cried out after Him, begging to be cured. The people tried to silence them with threats, but they followed Jesus, crying after Him: "Ah, Thou Son of David! Have mercy on us!" Then Jesus turned, commanded them to be led to Him, and touched their eyes. They saw and followed Him. A great tumult arose on account of the cure of these blind men, as well as of those to whom Jesus had restored sight on His entrance into Jericho. The Pharisees instituted an inquiry into the case, and interrogated the father of one of the cured, as well as himself. The disciples meantime were very desirous that Jesus should go to Lazarus' in Bethania, for there they would be in greater peace and less molested. They were in truth a little discontented, but Jesus went on curing numbers. Words cannot express how gentle and forbearing He was under such imputations, attacks and persecutions, and how sweetly and gravely He smiled when the disciples wanted to divert Him from His purpose. He next went in the direction of Samaria. Not far from one of the little villages along the highroad, about a hundred paces to one side, there stood a tent in which ten lepers were lying in beds. As Jesus was passing, the lepers came out and cried to Him for help. Jesus stood still, but the disciples went on. The lepers, entirely enveloped in their mantles, approached—some quickly, others slowly, as their strength permitted—and stood in a circle around Jesus. He touched each one separately, directed them to present themselves to the priests, and went on His way. One of the lepers, a Samaritan and the most active of the ten, went along the same road with two of the disciples, but the others took different routes. These were not cured all at once; although able to walk, they were not made perfectly clean till about an hour afterward.

(Vol. 3, pp. 476-477)

48. Lazarus' Death and Burial

The one leper returns to thank Jesus for his cure.
Jesus and His disciples are invited to a wedding
in a shepherd village, where He blesses the couple.
While Jesus is on His way to visit His Blessed Mother in
Samaria, Lazarus dies of his illness in Bethania.

As Jesus was tarrying in a little place near Samaria
where too the Blessed Virgin and Mary Cleophas were
come to spend the Sabbath, they received the news of
Lazarus' death. After this event, which happened in Bethania, his sisters left that place and went to their country
house near Ginaea, with the intention of there meeting
Jesus and the Blessed Virgin. The remains of Lazarus were
embalmed and swathed in linen bands, according to the
Jewish custom, and then laid in a coffin of woven rods with
a convex cover. All the apostles were again united around
Jesus. They went in several bands to Ginaea, where Jesus
taught in the synagogue and, after the closing exercises of
the Sabbath, went out to Lazarus' country house. There
they found the Blessed Virgin, who had gone on before.
Magdalen came to meet Jesus and to tell Him of her
brother's death, adding the words: "Lord, if Thou hadst
been here, my brother had not died!" Jesus replied that his
time was not yet come and that it was well that he had
died. Still He told the two sisters to allow all the effects of
their brother to remain at Bethania, for that He Himself
would go there shortly. The holy women, therefore, set out
for Bethania, while Jesus and the Apostles returned to
Ginaea, from which they went to the inn one hour distant
from Bethania. Here another messenger came to Him
bearing the earnest request of the sisters that He should
repair to Bethania, but He still delayed to go. He rebuked
the disciples for their murmuring and impatience at His
delaying so long to go to Bethania. He was always like one

who could not give an account of His views and actions to them, because they did not understand Him. In His instructions to them He was always more desirous of discovering to them their own thoughts and, on account of their earthly-mindedness, of arousing in them distrust of self than of informing them of the reasons of things that they could not comprehend. He still taught upon the laborers in the vineyard, and when the mother of James and John heard Him speak of the near fulfillment of His mission, she thought it only proper that His own relatives should have honorable posts in His Kingdom. She consequently approached Him with a petition to that effect, but He sternly rebuked her.   (Vol. 3, pp. 480-481)

49. Jesus Mourns with Martha and Magdalen

At last Jesus turned His steps to Bethania, continuing all along the way His instructions to the Apostles. Lazarus' estate stood partly within the walls surrounding the environs of the city, and partly—that is, a portion of the garden and courtyard—outside those walls, which were now going to ruin.

Lazarus was eight days dead. They had kept him four days in the hope that Jesus would come and raise him to life. His sisters, as I have said, went to the country house near Ginaea, to meet Jesus; but when they found that He was still resolved not to go back with them, they had returned to Bethania and buried their brother. Their friends, men and women from the city and from Jerusalem, were now gathered around them, lamenting the dead as was the custom. It seems to me that it was toward evening when Mary Zebedeus went in to Martha, who was sitting among the women, and said to her softly

that the Lord was coming. Martha arose and went out
with her into the garden back of the house. There in an
arbor was Magdalen sitting alone. Martha told her that
Jesus was near, for through love for Magdalen, she wanted
her to be the first to meet the Lord. But I did not see Magdalen go to Jesus, for when He was alone with the Apostles and disciples He did not allow women easy access to
Him. It was already growing dusk when Magdalen went
back to the women and took Martha's place, who then
went out to meet Jesus. He was standing with the Apostles and some others on the confines of their garden before
an open arbor. Martha spoke to Jesus and then turned
back to Magdalen, who also by this time had come up. She
threw herself at Jesus' feet, saying: "If Thou hadst been
here, he would not have died!" All present were in tears.
Jesus too mourned and wept, and delivered a discourse of
great length upon death. Many of the audience, which was
constantly increasing outside the bower, whispered to one
another and murmured their dissatisfaction at Jesus' not
having kept Lazarus alive.

(Vol. 3, pp. 481-482)

---

50. Jesus Raises Lazarus from the Dead

Early the next morning Jesus is taken to the tomb.
He is accompanied by the Apostles and
seven of the holy women, along with an
ever-increasing crowd of lookers-on.

Lazarus' tomb was the first on the right of the entrance
to the vault, down into which some steps led. It was a four-
cornered, oblong cave, about three feet in depth, and covered with a flat stone. In it lay the corpse in a lightly
woven coffin, and around it in the tomb there was room for
one to walk. Jesus with some of the Apostles went down

into the vault, while the holy women, Magdalen, and Martha remained standing in the doorway. But the crowd pressed around so that many people climbed up on the roof of the vault and the cemetery walls in order to see. Jesus commanded the Apostles to raise the stone from the grave. They did so, rested it against the wall, and then removed a light cover or door that closed the tomb below that stone. It was at this point of the proceedings that Martha said: "Lord, by this time he stinketh, for he is now of four days." After that they took the lightly woven cover from the coffin, and disclosed the corpse lying in its winding sheet. At that instant Jesus raised His eyes to Heaven, prayed aloud, and called out in a strong voice: "Lazarus, come forth!" At this cry, the corpse arose to a sitting posture. The crowd now pressed with so much violence that Jesus ordered them to be driven outside the walls of the cemetery. The Apostles, who were standing in the tomb by the coffin, removed the handkerchief from Lazarus' face, unbound his hands and feet, and drew off the winding sheet. Lazarus, as if waking from lethargy, rose from the coffin and stepped out of the grave, tottering and looking like a phantom. The Apostles threw a mantle around him. Like one walking in sleep, he approached the door, passed the Lord and went out to where his sisters and the other women had stepped back in fright as before a ghost. Without daring to touch him, they fell prostrate on the ground. At the same instant, Jesus stepped after him out of the vault and seized him by both hands, His whole manner full of loving earnestness.

And now all moved on toward Lazarus' house. The throng was great. but a certain fear prevailed among the people; consequently the procession formed by Lazarus and his friends was not impeded in its movements by the crowd that followed. Lazarus moved along more like one floating than walking, and he still had all the appearance of a corpse. Jesus walked by his side, and the rest of the party followed sobbing and weeping around them in silent, frightened amazement. They reached the old gate, and went along the road bordered by verdant hedges to the avenue of trees from which they had started. The Lord entered it with Lazarus and His followers, while the crowd thronged outside, clamoring and shouting.

At this moment Lazarus threw himself prostrate on the earth before Jesus, like one about to be received into a Religious Order. Jesus spoke some words, and then they went on to the house, about a hundred paces distant.

Jesus, the Apostles, and Lazarus were alone in the dining hall. The Apostles formed a circle around Jesus and Lazarus, who was kneeling before the Lord. Jesus laid His right hand on his head and breathed upon him seven times. The Lord's breath was luminous. I saw a dark vapor withdrawing as it were from Lazarus, and the devil under the form of a black winged figure, impotent and wrathful, clearing the circle backward and mounting on high. By this ceremony, Jesus consecrated Lazarus to His service, purified him from all connection with the world and sin, and strengthened him with the gifts of the Holy Ghost. He made him a long address in which He told him that He had raised him to life that he might serve Him, and that he would have to endure great persecution on the part of the Jews.

Up to this time, Lazarus was in his grave clothes, but now he retired to lay them aside and put on his own garments. It was at this moment that his sisters and friends embraced him for the first time, for before this there was something so corpselike about him that it inspired terror. I saw meanwhile that Lazarus' soul, during the time of its separation from his body, was in a place peaceful and painless, lighted by only a glimmering twilight, and that while there he related to the just, Joseph, Joachim, Anne,

Zachary, John, etc., how things were going with the Redeemer on earth.

By the Saviour's breathing upon him, Lazarus received the seven gifts of the Holy Ghost and was perfectly freed from connection with earthly things. He received those gifts before the Apostles, for he had by his death become acquainted with great mysteries, had gazed upon another world. He had actually been dead, and he was now born again. He could therefore receive those gifts. Lazarus comprises in himself a deep significance and a profound mystery.   (Vol. 3, pp. 483-485)

---

51. Jesus Teaches in Jericho and Elsewhere

From Bethania Jesus goes to Jerusalem with John and Matthew to visit and instruct His friends in the city. He takes leave of His disciples, telling them to meet Him at the end of three months at Jacob's Well, and taking with Him only three youths, He travels through the lands of the Three Kings. The Apostles and disciples disperse—some returning home, others traveling about the country teaching. Jesus returns with many new disciples and sends them to help the Apostles. He then travels to Ephron with the three youths, teaching at villages and farms along the way.

From Epron Jesus dispatched the three trusty disciples to meet the holy women who, to the number of ten, had reached the rented inn near Jericho. They were the Blessed Virgin, Magdalen, Martha, and two others, Peter's wife and stepdaughter, Andrew's wife, and Zacheus' wife and daughter. The last-mentioned was married to a very deserving disciple named Annadias, a shepherd and a relative of Silas' mother. Peter, Andrew, and John met Jesus on the road, and with them He went on to Jericho. The

Blessed Virgin, Magdalen, Martha, and others awaited His coming near a certain well. It was two hours before sundown when He came up with them. The women cast themselves on their knees before Him and kissed His hand. Mary also kissed His hand, and when she arose, Jesus kissed hers. Magdalen stood somewhat back. At the well, the disciples washed Jesus' feet, also those of the Apostles, after which all partook of a repast. The women ate alone and, when their meal was over, took their places at the lower end of the dining hall to listen to Jesus' words. He did not remain at the inn, but went with the three Apostles to Jericho, where the rest of the Apostles and disciples along with numerous sick were assembled. The women followed Him. I saw Him going into many of the houses and curing the sick, after which He Himself unlocked the school and ordered a chair to be placed in the center of the hall. The holy women were present in a retired part. They had a lamp to themselves. Mary was with them. After the instruction, the holy women went back to their inn and on the following morning returned to their homes. Crowds were gathered at Jericho, for Jesus' coming had been announced by the disciples. During His teaching and healing on the following day, the pressing and murmuring of the Pharisees were very great, and they sent messengers to Jerusalem to report. Jesus next went to the place of Baptism on the Jordan where were lying numbers of sick in expectation of His coming. They had heard of His reappearance and had begged His aid. There were little huts and tents around, under which they could descend into the water. I saw too the basin in the little island in which He had been baptized. Sometimes it was full, but again, the water was allowed to run off. They came from all parts for this water, from Samaria, Judea, Galilee, and even from Syria. They loaded asses with large leathern sacks of it. The sacks hung on either side of the beast, and were kept together over the animal's back by hoops. Jesus cured numbers. Only John, Andrew, and James the Less were with Him.   (Vol. 3, pp. 580-582)

---

52. Magdalen Perfumes Jesus' Hair

When the crowd became too great, Jesus went with the three Apostles to Bethel, where the Patriarch Jacob saw on a hill the ladder reaching from earth to Heaven. It was already dark when they arrived and approached a house wherein trusty friends were awaiting them: Lazarus and his sisters, Nicodemus, and John Marc, who had come hither from Jerusalem secretly. The master of the house had a wife and four children. The house was surrounded by a courtyard in which was a fountain. Attended by two of his children, the master opened the door to the guests, whom he conducted at once to the fountain and washed their feet. As Jesus was sitting on the edge of the fountain, Magdalen came forth from the house and poured over His hair a little flat flask of perfume. She did it standing at His back, as she had often done before. I wondered at her boldness. Jesus pressed to His heart Lazarus, who was still pale and haggard. His hair was very black. A meal was spread, consisting of fruit, rolls, honeycomb, and green herbs, the usual fare in Judea. There were little cups on the table. Jesus cured the sick who were lying in a building belonging to the house. The women ate alone and afterward ranged in the lower part of the hall to hear Jesus' preaching.   (Vol. 3, pp. 582-583)

---

53. The Apostles Are Reunited with Jesus

*Jesus and the three Apostles, John, Andrew and James
the Less, make their way to Capharnaum, teaching and
curing many on their way. From thence He and His
disciples head to the mountain of the multiplication of
the loaves to meet the other disciples and Apostles.*

One hour's distance from Thanath-Silo all the Apostles, bearing green branches, came to meet Jesus. They
prostrated before Him and He took one of the branches in
His hand. Then they washed His feet. I think this ceremony took place because they were all again reunited,
and because Jesus once more appeared openly as their
Master and was about to preach again everywhere.
Accompanied by the Apostles and disciples He went to
the city, where the Blessed Virgin, Magdalen, Martha,
and the other holy women, except Peter's wife and stepdaughter and Andrew's wife, who were still at Bethsaida,
received Him outside an inn. Mary had come from the
region of Jericho and had here awaited Jesus. The other
women also had come hither by different routes. They
prepared a meal of which fifty guests partook, after which
Jesus, having ordered the key to be brought, repaired to
the school. The holy women and a great many people lis-
tened to His instruction.   (Vol. 3, p. 587)

---

54. Jesus Instructs the New Disciples

*The next morning, Jesus cures many of the city of
Thanath-Silo. He and His disciples celebrate the
Sabbath at an inn on the way to Bethania.*

On the way to Bethania, Jesus, to continue His instructions for the benefit of the new disciples, explained to
them the *Our Father,* spoke to them of fidelity in His ser-

vice, and told them that He would now teach awhile in Jerusalem, after which He would soon return to His Heavenly Father. He told them also that one would abandon Him, for treason was already in his heart. All these new disciples remained faithful. On this journey, Jesus healed several lepers who had been brought out on the road. One hour from Bethania, they entered the inn at which Jesus had taught so long before Lazarus' resurrection and to which Magdalen had come forth to meet Him. The Blessed Virgin also was at the inn with other women, likewise five of the Apostles: Judas, Thomas, Simon, James the Less, Thaddeus, John Marc, and some others. Lazarus was not there. The Apostles came out a part of the way to meet the Lord at a well, where they saluted Him and washed His feet, after which He gave an instruction which was followed by a meal. The women then went on to Bethania while Jesus remained at the inn with the rest of the party. Next day, instead of going straight to Bethania, He made a circuit around the adjacent country with the three silent disciples. The rest of the Apostles and disciples separated into two bands, headed respectively by Thaddeus and James, and went around curing the sick. I saw them effecting cures in many different ways: by the imposition of hands, by breathing upon or leaning over the sick person, or in the case of children, by taking them on their knees, resting them on their breast and breathing upon them.   (Vol. 3, pp. 588-589)

55. Magdalen Prepares a Meal for
Jesus and His Disciples

*Jesus tells His Blessed Mother and the disciples of
His coming sufferings as well as the sufferings they
will endure after His death. Judas has decided to
betray Jesus to the Pharisees. After a fifteen-day stay at
the home of Lazarus, Jesus solemnly enters Jerusalem
riding on an ass. He is preceded by the twelve Apostles
and followed by the disciples and the holy women. The
streets of Jerusalem swarm with followers, friends and
the curious, who joyfully welcome Jesus, spreading their
mantles and palm branches on His way. Although the
distance from the Gate to the Temple is only about
a half hour, the procession takes three hours.*

By this time the Jews had ordered all the houses, as
well as the city gate, to be closed, so that when Jesus dis-
mounted before the Temple, and the disciples wanted to
take the ass back to where they had found it, they were
obliged to wait inside the gate till evening. In the Temple
were the holy women and crowds of people. All had to
remain the whole day without food, for this part of the city
had been barricaded. Magdalen was especially troubled by
the thought that Jesus had taken no nourishment.

When toward evening the gate was again opened, the
holy women went back to Bethania, and Jesus followed
later with the Apostles. Magdalen, worried because Jesus
and His followers had had no refreshment in Jerusalem,
now prepared a meal for them herself. It was already
dark when Jesus entered the courtyard of Lazarus'
dwelling. Magdalen brought Him a basin of water,
washed His feet, and dried them with a towel that was
hanging over her shoulder. The food that she had prepared did not amount to a regular meal, it was merely a
luncheon. While the Lord was partaking of it, she

VISIONS OF ANNE CATHERINE EMMERICH

approached and poured balm over His head. I saw Judas, who passed her at this moment, muttering his dissatisfaction, but she replied to his murmurs by saying that she could never thank the Lord sufficiently for what He had done for her and her brother. After that Jesus went to the public house of Simon the leper, where several of the disciples were gathered, and taught a little while. From there He went out to the disciples' inn, where He spoke for some time, and then returned to the house of Simon the leper. (Vol. 4, pp. 18-19)

56. Magdalen Repeats Her Anointing of Jesus

The next day Jesus teaches in the Temple, where He again drives out the merchants and vendors.

Full of trouble, Jesus went back with the Apostles to Bethania for the Sabbath. While He was teaching in the Temple, the Jews had been ordered to keep their houses closed, and it was forbidden to offer Him or His disciples any refreshment. On reaching Bethania, they went to the public house of Simon, the healed leper, where a meal awaited them. Magdalen, filled with compassion for Jesus' fatiguing exertions, met the Lord at the door. She was habited in a penitential robe and girdle, her flowing hair concealed by a black veil. She cast herself at His feet and with her hair wiped from them the dust, just as one would clean the shoes of another. She did it openly before all, and many were scandalized at her conduct.

After Jesus and the disciples had prepared themselves for the Sabbath, that is, put on the garments prescribed and prayed under the lamp, they stretched themselves at table for the meal. Toward the end of it, Magdalen, urged by love, gratitude, contrition, and anxiety, again made her appearance. She went behind the Lord's couch, broke a

little flask of precious balm over His head and poured
some of it upon His feet, which she again wiped with her
hair. That done, she left the dining hall. Several of those
present were scandalized, especially Judas, who excited
Matthew, Thomas, and John Mark to displeasure. But
Jesus excused her, on account of the love she bore Him.
She often anointed Him in this way. Many of the facts
mentioned only once in the Gospels happened frequently.
(Vol. 4, pp. 21-22)

57. The Holy Women at Prayer

While Jesus was teaching in Jerusalem, I saw the holy
women frequently praying together in the arbor in which
Magdalen was sitting when Martha called her to welcome
Jesus before the raising of Lazarus. They observed a certain order at prayer: sometimes they stood together, sometimes they knelt, or again they sat apart.   (Vol. 4, p. 25)

58. Jesus Reproves the Disciples for Being Scandalized at Magdalen

Judas contacts Caiaphas in his first treacherous step.
Jesus is in the Temple daily, teaching in parables and
answering questions. He sends His disciples two by two
into the surrounding area to teach and heal. In the
evenings, they are invited to rest at the houses of friends
and followers. Jesus warns the Apostles and disciples
that one of them will betray Him into the hands of
His enemies and that all of them will desert Him.

Jesus exhorted the Apostles not to give way to their natural fears upon what He had said to them, namely, that
they would all be dispersed; they should not forget their

neighbor and should not allow one sentiment to veil, to stifle another; and here He made use of the similitude of a mantle. In general terms He reproached some of them for murmuring at Magdalen's anointing. Jesus probably said this in reference to Judas' first definitive step toward His betrayal, which had been taken just after that action of hers—also, as a gentle warning to him for the future, since it would be after Magdalen's last anointing that he would carry out his treacherous design. That some others were scandalized at Magdalen's prodigal expression of love, arose from their erroneous severity and parsimony. They regarded this anointing as a luxury so often abused at worldly feasts, while overlooking the fact that such an action performed on the Holy of Holies was worthy of the highest praise.   (Vol. 4, pp. 31-32)

---

59. Magdalen Procures the Precious Balm

The Pharisees take turns to spy on Jesus and His
disciples. After this day's teaching in the Temple,
Jesus spends the evening at the home of Lazarus,
where He tells His disciples that they may have one
more night of peaceful sleep. He gives instruction
in the Temple for the last time and tells the Apostles
and disciples that He will never enter there again.
All of His followers become anxious and saddened.
They stay the night at Lazarus' in Bethania.

Next morning Jesus instructed a large number of the disciples, more than sixty, in the court before Lazarus' house. In the afternoon, about three o'clock, tables were laid for them in the court, and during their meal Jesus and the Apostles served. I saw Jesus going from table to table handing something to this one, something to that, and teaching all the time. Judas was not present. He was away making purchases for the entertainment to be given at Simon's. Magdalen also had gone to Jerusalem, to buy precious ointment. The Blessed Virgin, to whom Jesus had that morning announced His approaching death, was inexpressibly sad. Her niece, Mary Cleophas, was always around her, consoling her. Full of grief, they went together to the disciples' inn.

It was during this instruction that Magdalen came back from Jerusalem with the ointment she had brought. She had gone to Veronica's and stayed there while Veronica saw to the purchase of the ointment, which was of three kinds, the most precious that could be procured. Magdalen had expended upon it all the money she had left. One was a flask of the oil of spikenard. She bought the flasks together with their contents. The former were of a clear, whitish, though not transparent material, almost like mother-of-pearl, though not mother-of-pearl. They were in shape like little urns, the swelling base ornamented with knobs, and they had screw tops. Magdalen carried the vessels under her mantle in a pocket, which hung on her breast suspended by a cord that passed over one shoulder and back across the back. John Mark's mother went back with her to Bethania, and Veronica accompanied them a part of the way. As they were going through Bethania, they met Judas who, concealing his indignation, spoke to Magdalen. Magdalen had heard from Veronica that the Pharisees had resolved to arrest Jesus and put Him to death, but not yet, on account of the crowds of strangers and especially the numerous pagans that followed Him. This news Magdalen imparted to the other women.(V o l . 4, pp. 41-43)

---

60. Magdalen's Last Anointing of Jesus

*Judas has purchased everything necessary for this
evening's meal, secretly thinking that he will be paid
tonight. The entertainment is given by Simon at his
public house in Bethania.*

Several large drinking glasses stood on the table, and
beside each, two smaller ones. There were three kinds of
beverages: one greenish, another red, and the third yellow. I think it was some kind of pear juice. The lamb was
served first. It lay stretched out on an oval dish, the head
resting on the forefeet. The dish was placed with the head
toward Jesus. Jesus took a white knife, like bone or stone,
inserted it into the back of the lamb, and cut, first to one
side of the neck and then to the other. After that He drew
the knife down, making a cut from the head along the
whole back. The lines of this cut, at once reminded me of
the Cross. He then laid the slices thus detached before
John, Peter and Himself, and directed Simon, the host, to
carve the lamb down the sides, and lay the pieces right
and left before the Apostles and Lazarus as they sat in
order.

The holy women were seated around their own table.
Magdalen, who was in tears all the time, sat opposite the
Blessed Virgin. There were seven or nine present. They
too had a little lamb. It was smaller than that of the other
table and lay stretched out flat in the dish, the head
toward the Mother of God. She it was who carved it.

Jesus taught during the whole meal. It was nearing the
close of His discourse; the Apostles were stretched forward
in breathless attention. Simon, whose services were no
longer needed, sat motionless, listening to every word,
when Magdalen rose quietly from her seat among the holy
women. She had around her a thin, bluish-white mantle,
something like the material worn by the three Holy Kings,

and her flowing hair was covered with a veil. Laying the ointment in a fold of her mantle, she passed through the walk that was planted with shrubbery, entered the hall, went up behind Jesus, and cast herself down at His feet, weeping bitterly. She bent her face low over the foot that was resting on the couch, while Jesus Himself raised to her the other that was hanging a little toward the floor. Magdalen loosened the sandals and anointed Jesus' feet on the soles and upon the upper part. Then with both hands drawing her flowing hair from beneath her veil, she wiped the Lord's anointed feet, and replaced the sandals. Magdalen's action caused some interruption in Jesus' discourse. He had observed her approach, but the others were taken by surprise. Jesus said: "Be not scandalized at this woman!" and then addressed some words softly to her. She now arose, stepped behind Him and poured over His head some costly water, and that so plentifully that it ran down upon His garments. Then with her hand she spread some of the ointment from the crown down the hind part of His head. The hall was filled with delicious odor. The Apostles whispered together and muttered their displeasure—even Peter was vexed at the interruption. Magdalen, weeping and veiled, withdrew around behind the table. When she was about to pass before Judas, he stretched forth his hand to stay her while he indignantly addressed to her some words on her extravagance, saying that the purchase money might have been given to the poor. Magdalen made no reply. She was weeping bitterly. Then Jesus spoke, bidding them let her pass, and saying that she had anointed Him for His death, for later she would not be able to do it, and that wherever this Gospel would be preached, her action and their murmuring would also be recounted.   (Vol. 4, pp. 44-46)

61. Judas

Judas was very dear and quite useful to his old uncle in his leather trade. Sometimes he dispatched him with asses to purchase raw hides, sometimes with prepared leather to the seaport towns, for he was a clever and cunning broker and commission merchant. Still he was not at this time a villain, and had he overcome himself in little things, he would not have fallen so low. The Blessed Virgin very often warned him, but he was extremely vacillating. He was susceptible of very vehement, though not lasting repentance. His head was always running on the establishment of an earthly kingdom, and when he found that not likely to be fulfilled, he began to appropriate the money entrusted to his care. He was therefore greatly vexed that the worth of Magdalen's ointment had not passed as alms through his hands. It was at the last Feast of Tabernacles in Jesus' lifetime that Judas began to go to the bad. When he betrayed Jesus for money, he never dreamed of His being put to death. He thought his Master would soon be released; his only desire was to make a little money.   (Vol. 2, p. 431)

62. Judas' Betrayal

Magdalen retired, her heart full of sorrow. The rest of the meal was disturbed by the displeasure of the Apostles and the reproaches of Jesus. When it was over, all returned to Lazarus'. Judas, full of wrath and avarice, thought within himself that he could no longer put up with such things. But concealing his feelings, he laid aside his festal garment and pretended that he had to go back to the public house to see that what remained of the meal was given to the poor. Instead of doing that, however, he ran full speed to Jerusalem. I saw the devil with him all the time, red, thin-bodied, and angular. He was before him and behind him, as

if lighting the way for him. Judas saw through the darkness. He stumbled not, but ran along in perfect safety. I saw
him in Jerusalem running into the house in which, later on,
Jesus was exposed to scorn and derision. The Pharisees and
High Priests were still together, but Judas did not enter
their assembly. Two of them went out and spoke with him
below in the courtyard. When he told them that he was
ready to deliver Jesus and asked what they would give for
Him, they showed great joy, and returned to announce it to
the rest of the council. After a while, one came out again
and made an offer of thirty pieces of silver. Judas wanted to
receive them at once, but they would not give them to him.
They said . . . that he should do his duty, and then they
would pay him. I saw them offering hands as a pledge of the
contract, and on both sides tearing something from their
clothing. The Pharisees wanted Judas to stay a while and
tell them when and how the bargain would be completed.
But he insisted upon going, that suspicion might not be
excited. He said that he had yet to find things out more precisely, that next day he could act without attracting attention. I saw the devil the whole time between Judas and the
Pharisees. On leaving Jerusalem, Judas ran back again to
Bethania, where he changed his garments and joined the
other Apostles.   (Vol. 4, pp. 46-47)

-----

63. "She Loves Unspeakably"

*Jesus takes His rest at Lazarus' that night, while His
followers retire to their own inn. The next morning
Jesus asks Peter and John to make preparations for the
Paschal Supper. Jesus and nine of the Apostles take
leave of Lazarus and the holy women in Bethania.*

I saw Him speaking alone with His Blessed Mother, and
I remember some of the words that passed between them.

He had, He said, sent Peter the Believing and John the Loving to Jerusalem in order to prepare for the Pasch. Of Magdalen, who was quite out of herself from grief, He said: "She loves unspeakably, but her love is still encompassed by the body, therefore has she become like one quite out of her mind with pain." He spoke also of the treacherous scheming of Judas, and the Blessed Virgin implored mercy for him.   (Vol. 4, p. 55)

---

64. The Blessed Virgin, Magdalen and Mary Cleophas Beseech Jesus Not to Go to Mount Olivet

Judas spends the whole day running between the Pharisees and cementing his plans with them. At midday Jesus and the nine leave Bethania and walk to Jerusalem, where they meet Peter and John at the Cenacle. Jesus immolates the Paschal lamb and signs the lintel and doorposts with its blood. Judas arrives as the Paschal lambs are being roasted. As they are eating the Paschal lamb, Jesus again warns them that one of them will betray Him. He washes the feet of the Apostles. He institutes the Blessed Sacrament. After Judas sacrilegiously receives the Holy Eucharist, he leaves the Caenaculum and runs to the Pharisees. Jesus ordains Peter and John. He tells Peter that even he will deny Him. They recite the Hymn of Thanksgiving and go into the anteroom.

Here Jesus met His Mother, Mary Cleophas, and Magdalen, who besought Him imploringly not to go to the Mount of Olives, for it was reported that He would there be arrested. Jesus comforted them in a few words, and stepped quickly past them. It was then about nine o'clock.

They went in haste down the road by which Peter and
John had come up that morning to the Cenacle, and
directed their steps to Mount Olivet.   (Vol. 4, p. 76)

---

65. Satan Accuses Jesus in the Garden of Olives

*Jesus and the eleven walk to Mount Olivet. Jesus bids
eight of the Apostles to stay in the Garden of Gethsemani
while He, Peter, John and James the Greater continue
on to the Garden of Olives. Jesus begs these three
to watch and pray with Him. He walks a little way
from them and is shown all the sins of mankind,
from the beginning of the world to the end.*

When now this enormous mass of sin and iniquity had
passed before the soul of Jesus in an ocean of horrible
visions and He had offered Himself as the expiatory sacrifice for all, had implored that all their punishment and
chastisement might fall upon Him, Satan, as once before
in the desert, brought forward innumerable temptations
against the innocent Saviour Himself. "What!" said he to
Him, "wilt Thou take all this upon Thee, and Thou art not
pure Thyself? See, here and here and here!" And he
unfolded all kinds of forged bonds and notes before Him,
and with infernal impudence held them up under His
eyes. He reproached Him with all the faults of His disciples, all the scandal they had given, all the disturbances
and disorder He had caused in the world by abolishing
ancient customs. Satan acted like the most crafty and
subtle Pharisee. He reproached Jesus with causing
Herod's massacre of the Holy Innocents, with exposing
His parents to want and danger in Egypt, with not having rescued John the Baptist from death, with bringing
about disunion in many families, with having protected

degraded people, refusing to cure certain sick persons, with injuring the Gergeseans by permitting the possessed to overturn their vats and their swine to rush into the sea. He accused Him of the guilt of Mary Magdalen, since He had not prevented her relapse into sin; of neglecting His own family; of squandering the goods of others; and, in one word, all that the tempter would at the hour of death have brought to bear upon an ordinary mortal who, without a high and holy intention, had been mixed up in such affairs, Satan now suggested to the trembling soul of Jesus with the view of causing Him to waver. It was hidden from him that Jesus was the Son of God, and he tempted Him as merely the most righteous of men. Yes, our Divine Redeemer permitted, in a certain measure, His most holy Humanity to veil His Divinity, that He might endure those temptations that come upon the holiest souls at the hour of death respecting the intrinsic merit of their good works. That He might drain the chalice of suffering, He permitted the tempter, from whom His Divinity was hidden, to upbraid Him with His works of beneficence as so many sins incurring penalty and not yet blotted out by the grace of God. The tempter reproached Him likewise for desiring to atone for the sins of others, although He was Himself without merit and had not yet made satisfaction to God for the grace of many a so-called good work. The Divinity of Jesus allowed the wicked fiend to tempt His Sacred Humanity just as he would tempt a man who might have ascribed his good works to some special merit of their own, independent of that which they can acquire by being united with the merits of the saving death of our Lord and Saviour. Thus, the tempter called up before Jesus all the works of His love as not only without merit for Himself, but as so many crimes against God; and as their value was, in a certain measure, derived from the merits of His

Passion not yet perfected and of whose worth Satan was ignorant, therefore for the grace by which He effected them, He had not yet made satisfaction. For all His good works, Satan showed Jesus written bonds, telling Him as he pointed to them: "For this action and for this also, hast Thou incurred indebtedness." At last he unrolled before Him a note that He had received from Lazarus for the sale of Magdalen's property in Magdalum, and the proceeds of which He had expended. Satan accompanied the action with these words: "How darest Thou squander the property of others and thereby injure the family?"

It was with the greatest difficulty that I restrained myself while all these charges were brought against the innocent Saviour. I was so enraged against Satan. But when he exhibited the note holding Jesus amendable for distributing the proceeds of Magdalen's property, I could no longer subdue my anger, and I exclaimed: "How canst thou charge Jesus with the sale of Magdalen's property as with a crime? I saw myself how the Lord devoted that sum received from Lazarus to works of mercy, how He released with it twenty-seven poor, abandoned creatures held prisoners for debt at Tirzah."   (Vol. 4, pp. 82-84)

66. Jesus' Followers during His Agony in the Garden

Jesus, overcome by sorrow and agony, returns
to the three, who, being exhausted by grief and
temptation, have fallen asleep. He awakens them,
they, seeing Him so disfigured by pain and agony,
become alarmed. They wish to call the other Apostles,
but Jesus refuses and prays with them for a short while.
He returns to the grotto and is shown all of the
ingratitude, the blasphemies and the negligences to be
committed against Him in the Holy Eucharist.

There was little bustle in Jerusalem on this evening. The Jews were in their homes busied with preparations for the feast. The lodgings for the Paschal guests were not in the neighborhood of the Mount of Olives. As I went to and fro on the road, I saw here and there friends and disciples of Jesus walking together and conversing. They appeared to be uneasy and in expectation of something. The Mother of the Lord, with Magdalen, Martha, Mary Cleophas, Mary Salome, and Salome had gone from the Cenacle to the house of Mary Marcus. Alarmed at the reports that she had heard, Mary and her friends went on toward the city to get some news of Jesus. Here they were met by Lazarus, Nicodemus, Joseph of Arimathea, and some relatives from Hebron, who sought to comfort Mary in her great anxiety. These friends knew of Jesus' earnest discourse in the Cenacle, some from being themselves present in the side buildings, others from having informed of it by the disciples; but although they questioned some Pharisees of their acquaintance, yet they heard of no immediate steps against Our Lord. They said, therefore, "The danger is not so great. And besides, the enemies of Jesus would make no attempt against Him so near to the feast." They did not know of Judas' treachery.

Mary told them how restless he had been during the past few days, and of his sudden departure from the Cenacle. He had certainly gone with treacherous intentions, for, as she said, she had often warned him that he was a son of perdition. The holy women returned to the house of Mary Marcus. (Vol. 4, p. 87)

---

67. In the Garden of Olives

I now saw the blood in thick, dark drops trickling down the pale face of the Lord. His once smoothly parted hair was matted with blood, tangled and bristling on His head, and His beard was bloody and torn. It was after that last vision, in which the armed bands had lacerated His flesh, that He turned as if fleeing out of the grotto, and went again to His disciples. But His step was far from secure. He walked bowed like one tottering under a great burden. He was covered with wounds, and He fell at every step. When He reached the three Apostles, He did not, as on the first occasion, find them lying on their side asleep; they had sunk back on the knees with covered head, as I have often seen the people of that country sitting when in sorrow or in prayer. Worn out with grief, anxiety, and fatigue, they had fallen asleep; but when Jesus approached, trembling and groaning, they awoke. They gazed upon Him with their weary eyes, but did not at once recognize Him, for He was changed beyond the power of words to express. He was standing before them in the moonlight, His breast sunken, His form bent, His face pale and bloodstained, His hair in disorder, and His arms stretched out to them. He stood wringing His hands. The Apostles sprang up, grasped Him under the arms, and supported Him tenderly. Then He spoke to them in deep affliction. On the morrow, He said, He was going to die. In another hour, His enemies would seize Him, drag Him before the courts of justice, abuse Him, deride Him, scourge Him, and put Him to death in the most horrible manner. He begged them to console His Mother. He recounted to them in bitter anguish all that He would have to suffer until the evening of the next day, and again begged them to comfort His Mother and Magdalen. He stood thus speaking for some moments, but the Apostles kept silence, not knowing what to reply. They were so filled with grief and consternation at His words, and appearance that they knew not what to say; indeed, they even thought that His mind was wandering. When He wanted to return to the grotto, He had not the power to do so. I saw that John and James had to lead Him. When He entered it, the Apostles left Him and went back to their own place. It was then a quarter past eleven.   (Vol. 4, pp. 102-103)

---

68. Jesus' Compassion for His Blessed Mother and Magdalen

During this agony of Jesus, I saw the Blessed Virgin overwhelmed with sorrow and anguish in the house of Mary Marcus. She was with Magdalen and Mary Marcus in a garden adjoining the house. She had sunk on her knees on a stone slab. She was perfectly absorbed in her own interior, quite diverted in thought from everything around her, seeing only, feeling only the sufferings of her Divine Son. She had sent messengers to obtain news of Him, but unable to await their coming, in her anguish of heart she went with Magdalen and Salome out into the Valley of Josaphat. I saw her walking along veiled, her arms often outstretched toward the Mount of Olives, where she saw in spirit Jesus agonizing and sweating blood. It seemed as if she would with her outstretched hands wipe

His sacred face. In answer to these interior and vehement movements of her soul toward her Son, I saw that Jesus was stirred with thoughts of her. He turned His eyes in her direction as if seeking help from her. I saw this mutual sympathy under the appearance of rays of light passing to and fro between them. The Lord thought also of Magdalen and felt for her in her distress. He glanced toward her, and His soul was touched at sight of her. He therefore ordered the disciples to console her, for He knew that her love for Him, after that of His Mother, was greater than that of anyone else. He saw what she would have to suffer for Him in the future, and also that she would never more offend Him.   (Vol. 4, pp. 103-104)

---

69. Jesus Is Shown His Passion

Jesus overcomes His human repugnance for suffering and is consoled by angels who show Him the ardent desires of the souls in Limbo, and multitudes of future Saints. He sees all the good works done for the love of Him, all the hardships endured and labors accomplished as the fruits of His sufferings.

But now these consoling pictures disappeared, and the angels displayed before His eyes all the scenes of His approaching Passion. They appeared quite close to the earth, for the time was near at hand. There were many angelic actors in these scenes. I beheld everyone close to Jesus, from the kiss of Judas to His own last words upon the Cross. I saw all, all there again, as I am accustomed to see it in my meditations upon the Passion. The treason of Judas, the flight of the disciples, the mockery and sufferings before Annas and Caiaphas, Peter's denial, Pilate's tribunal, Herod's derision, the scourging and crowning with thorns, the condemnation to death, the sinking under the weight of the Cross, the meeting with the Blessed Virgin and her swooning, the jeers of the executioners against her, Veronica's handkerchief, the cruel nailing to the Cross and the raising of the same, the insults of the Pharisees, the sorrows of Mary, of Magdalen, and of John, and the piercing of His side—in a word, all, all, clearly, significantly, and in their minutest details passed before Him. All the gestures, all the sentiments, and words of His future tormentors, I saw that the Lord beheld and heard in alarm and anguish of soul. He willingly accepted all, He willingly submitted to all through love for man. He was most painfully troubled at His shameful stripping on the Cross, which He endured to atone for the immodesty of men, and He implored that He might retain a girdle at least upon the Cross, but even this was not allowed Him. I saw, however, that He was to receive help, not from the executioners, but from a certain good person.(Vol. 4, 106-107)

70. Judas and the Pharisees

An angel offers Jesus the chalice and He, accepting this chalice of His Passion, drinks from it, receiving new strength. He walks with a firm step to the three Apostles, who have again fallen asleep. "Arise, let us go! Behold, the traitor is approaching! Oh, it were better for him had he never been born!"

At the beginning of his treasonable career, Judas had really never looked forward to the result that followed upon it. He wanted to obtain the traitor's reward and please the Pharisees by pretending to deliver Jesus into their hands, but he had never counted on things going so far, he never dreamed of Jesus' being brought to judgment and crucified. He was thinking only of the money,

and he had for a long time been in communication with
some sneaking, spying Pharisees and Sadducees who by
flattery were inciting him to treason. He was tired of
the fatiguing, wandering, and persecuted life led by the
Apostles. For several months past, he had begun this
downward course by stealing the alms committed to his
care; and his avarice, excited by Magdalen's lavish
anointing of Jesus, urged him on to extremes. He had
always counted upon Jesus' establishing a temporal kingdom in which he hoped for some brilliant and lucrative
post. But as this was not forthcoming, he turned his
thoughts to amassing a fortune. He saw that hardships
and persecution were on the increase; and so he thought
that, before things came to the worst, he would ingratiate
himself with some of the powerful and distinguished
among Jesus' enemies. He saw that Jesus did not become
a king; whereas, the High Priests and prominent men of
the Temple were people very attractive in his eyes. And so
he allowed himself to be drawn into closer communication with their agents, who flattered him in every way
and told him in the greatest confidence that under any
circumstances an end would soon be put to Jesus' career.
During the last few days they followed him to Bethania,
and thus he continued to sink deeper and deeper into
depravity. He almost ran his legs off to induce the High
Priests to come to some conclusion. But they would not
come to terms and treated him with great contempt. They
told him that the time now intervening before the feast
was too short. If any action were taken now, it would create trouble and disturbance on the feast. The Sanhedrin
alone paid some degree of attention to his proposals.
After his sacrilegious reception of the Sacrament, Satan
took entire possession of him and he went off at once to
complete his horrible crime. He first sought those agents
who had until now constantly flattered him and received

him with apparent friendship. Some others joined the party, among them Caiaphas and Annas, but the last-named treated him very rudely and scornfully. They were irresolute and mistrustful of the consequences, nor did they appear to place any confidence in Judas.

(Vol. 4, pp. 109-110)

---

71. Jesus' Followers Learn of His Arrest

Judas persuades the Pharisees to arrest Jesus now and receives his thirty pieces of silver. He leads the soldiers to the Garden of Olives, where he betrays Jesus with a kiss. Jesus is taken into custody. The Apostles and disciples, being frightened and confused, run away and hide. On the way to Jerusalem, Jesus is violently abused and mistreated. He is dragged over sharp stones and beaten with prods and whips. As the party is about to enter Ophel, it is joined by fifty more soldiers, since Jesus has many followers here.

When this shouting band hurried from Ophel by torch-light to meet the approaching procession, the disciples lurking around dispersed in all directions. I saw that the Blessed Virgin, in her trouble and anguish, with Martha, Magdalen, Mary Cleophas, Mary Salome, Mary Marcus, Susanna, Johanna Chusa, Veronica, and Salome, again directed her steps to the Valley of Josaphat. They were to the south of Gethsemani, opposite that part of Mount Olivet where was another grotto in which Jesus had formerly been accustomed to pray. I saw Lazarus, John Mark, Veronica's son, and Simeon's son with them. The last-named, along with Nathanael, had been in Gethsemani with the eight Apostles, and had fled across when the tumult began. They brought news to the Blessed Virgin. Meanwhile they heard the cries and saw the torches of the two bands as they met. The Blessed Virgin was in uninterrupted contemplation of Jesus' torments and sympathetic suffering with her Divine Son. She allowed the holy women to lead her back part of the way so that, when the tumultuous procession should have passed, she might again return to the house of Mary Marcus.   (Vol. 4, p. 125)

---

72. The Soldiers Mock Magdalen's Anointing of Jesus

The inhabitants of Ophel, seeing Jesus, bound and bloody, being led by soldiers, cry and lament for the Prophet who has cured and taught so many. Jesus is taken to the palace of Annas, where He is accused and insulted. He is then taken to the judgment hall of Caiaphas. John and Peter make their way into the council area among the servants and soldiers. Caiaphas accuses Jesus of blasphemy and delivers Him to the executioners, who take turns beating Him, stabbing Him with needles and tearing His hair and beard, viciously abusing Him.

When they covered Jesus with mud and spittle, the vile miscreants exclaimed: "Here now is Thy royal unction, Thy prophetic unction!" It was thus they mockingly alluded to Magdalen's anointing and to Baptism. "What!" they cried jeeringly, "art Thou going to appear before the Sanhedrin in this unclean trim? Thou wast wont to purify others, and yet Thou art not clean Thyself. But we will now purify Thee." Thereupon, they brought a basin full of foul, muddy water in which lay a coarse rag; and amid pushes, jests, and mockery mingled with ironical bows and salutations, with sticking out the tongue at Him or turning up to Him their hinder parts, they passed the wet smeary rag over His face and shoulders as if cleansing Him, though in reality rendering Him more filthy than before. Finally, they poured the whole contents of the basin over His face with the mocking words: "There, now, is precious balm for Thee! There now, Thou hast nard water at a cost of three hundred pence! Now, Thou hast Thy baptism of the Pool of Bethsaida!"

(Vol. 4, pp. 156-157)

73. "O Thou Most Unhappy Mother!"

John, horrified and fearing that the Blessed Virgin might hear of these things from strangers, leaves the judgment hall to seek her at the home of Martha. Peter, unable to abandon his Lord, but also unable to watch the abuses loaded upon Him, seeks a corner in the atrium by a fire. He thrice denies Jesus and, hearing the cock crow a second time, realizes the enormity of his fault. He covers his head with his mantle, shedding bitter tears.

The Blessed Virgin, united in constant, interior compassion with Jesus, knew and experienced in her soul all that happened to Him. She suffered everything with Him in spiritual contemplation, and like Him she was absorbed in continual prayer for His executioners. But at the same time, her mother-heart cried uninterruptedly to God that He might not suffer these crimes to be enacted, that He might ward off these sufferings from her Most Blessed Son, and she irresistibly longed to be near her poor, out-raged Jesus. When then John, after the frightful cry: "He is guilty of death!" left the court of Caiaphas and went to her at Lazarus' in Jerusalem, not far from the corner gate; and when, by his account of the terrible sufferings of her Son, he confirmed what she already well knew from inte-rior contemplation, she ardently desired to be conducted together with Magdalen (who was almost crazed from grief), and some others of the holy women, to where she might be near her suffering Jesus. John, who had left the presence of His Divine Master only to console her who was next to Jesus with him, accompanied the Blessed Virgin when led by the holy women from the house. Magdalen, wringing her hands, staggered with the others along the moonlit streets, which were alive with people returning to their homes. The holy women were veiled. But their little party, closely clinging to one another, their occasional sobs and expressions of grief, which could not be restrained, drew upon them the notice of the passers-by, many of whom were Jesus' enemies; and the bitter, abusive words which they heard uttered against the Lord added to their pain. The most afflicted Mother suffered in constant, interior contemplation the torments of Jesus, which, however, like all other things, she quietly kept in her heart; for, like Him, she suffered with Him in silence. The holy women supported her in their arms. When passing under an arched gateway of the inner city, through which their way led, they were met by some well-disposed people returning from Caiaphas' judgment hall and lamenting the scenes they had witnessed. They approached the holy women and, recognizing the Mother of Jesus, paused a moment to salute her with heartfelt compassion: "O thou most unhappy Mother! Thou most afflicted Mother! O thou most distressed Mother of the Holy One of Israel!" Mary thanked them earnestly, and the holy women with hurried steps continued their sorrowful way. (Vol. 4, pp. 162-163)

---

74. Peter Confesses to Mary His Denial of Jesus

When now they reached the outer court of the house,

Mary, in the midst of the holy women and accompanied by John, withdrew into a corner under the gateway leading into the inner court. Her soul, filled with inexpressible sufferings, was with Jesus. She sighed for the door to be opened, and hoped, through John's intervention, to be allowed admittance. She felt that this door alone separated her from her Son who, at the second crowing of the cock, was to be led out of the house and into the prison below. At last the door opened and Peter, weeping bitterly, his head covered and his hands outstretched, rushed to meet the crowd issuing forth. The glare of the torches, added to the light shed by the moon, enabled him at once to recognize John and the Blessed Virgin. It seemed to him that conscience, which the glance of the Son had roused and terrified, stood before him in the person of the Mother. Oh, how the soul of poor Peter quivered when Mary accosted him with "O Simon, what about my Son, what about Jesus?" Unable to speak or to support the glance of Mary's eyes, Peter turned away wringing his hands. But Mary would not desist. She approached him and said in a voice full of emotion: "O Simon, son of Cephas, thou answerest me not?" Thereupon in the deepest woe, Peter exclaimed: "O Mother, speak not to me! Thy Son is suffering cruelly. Speak not to me! They have condemned Him to death, and I have shamefully denied Him thrice!" And when John drew near to speak to him, Peter, like one crazed by grief, hurried out of the court and fled from the city. He paused not until he reached that cave on Mount Olivet upon whose stones were impressed the marks of Jesus' hands while He prayed. In the same cave our first father Adam did penance, for it was here that he first reached the curse-laden earth.

The Blessed Virgin, in compassion for Jesus in this new pain, that of being denied by the disciple who had been the first to acknowledge Him the Son of the Living God, at these words of Peter, sank down upon the stone pavement upon which she was standing by the pillar of the gateway. The marks of her hand or foot remained impressed upon the stone, which is still in existence, though I do not remember where I have seen it. Most of the crowd had dispersed after Jesus was imprisoned, and the gate of the court was still standing open. Rising from where she had fallen and longing to be nearer her beloved Son, John conducted the Blessed Virgin and the holy women to the front of the Lord's prison. Mary was indeed with Jesus in spirit and knew all that was happening to Him, and He too was with her. But this most faithful Mother wished to hear with her bodily ears the sighs of her Son. She could in her present position hear both the sighs of Jesus and the insults heaped upon Him. The little group could not here remain long unobserved. Magdalen was too greatly agitated to conquer the vehemence of her grief, and though the Blessed Virgin by a special grace appeared wonderfully dignified and venerable in her exterior manifestation of her exceedingly great suffering, yet even while going this short distance she was obliged to listen to words of bitter import, such as: "Is not this the Galilean's Mother? Her Son will certainly be crucified, though not before the festival, unless, indeed He is the greatest of criminals." The Blessed Virgin turned and, guided by the Spirit that enlightened her interiorly, went to the fireplace in the atrium where only a few of the rabble were still standing. Her companions followed in speechless grief. In this place of horror, where Jesus had declared that He was the Son of God and where the brood of Satan had cried out: "He is guilty of death," the most afflicted Mother's anguish was so great that she appeared more like a dying than a living person. John and the holy women led her away from the spot. The lookers-on became silent, as if stupefied. The effect produced by Mary's presence was what might be caused by a pure spirit passing through Hell.

(Vol. 4, pp. 164-166)

---

75. Mary, John and Magdalen at Pilate's Tribunal

Jesus is imprisoned for the night. Judas is told that Jesus has been condemned to death, but he is resolved to await the outcome of the morning trial. Shortly after sunrise, Jesus is again brought before the council, where He again admits to being the Son of God. He is then led to the palace of Pilate. On the way, Judas overhears that Jesus is indeed condemned to death. He runs to the Temple and tries to give back the money, but is put off with scorn. He becomes as one insane, casts the silver onto the floor of the Temple and flees the city. Overcome by despair, he hangs himself on a tree at the foot of the Mount of Scandals.

Not very far from the house of Caiaphas, crowded together in the corner of a building, and waiting for the coming procession, were the blessed and afflicted Mother of Jesus, Magdalen, and John. Mary's soul was always with Jesus, but wherever she could approach Him in body also, her love gave her no rest. It drove her out upon His path and into His footsteps. After her midnight visit to Caiaphas' tribunal, she had in speechless grief tarried only a short time in the Cenacle; for scarcely was Jesus led forth from prison for the morning trial, when she too arose. Enveloped in mantle and veil and taking the lead of John and Magdalen, she said: "Let us follow My Son to Pilate. My eyes must again behold Him." Taking a bypath, they got in advance of the procession, and here the Blessed Virgin stood and waited along with the others. The Mother of Jesus knew how things were going with her Son. Her soul had Him always before her eyes, but that interior view could never have depicted Him so disfigured and maltreated as He really was by the wickedness of human creatures. She did, in truth, see constantly His frightful sufferings, but all aglow with the light of His love and His sanctity, with the glory of that patient endurance with which He was accomplishing His sacrifice. But now passed before her gaze the frightful reality in all its ignoble significance. The proud and enraged enemies of Jesus, the High Priests of the true God in their robes of ceremony, full of malice, fraud, falsehood and blasphemy, passed before her, revolving deicidal designs. The priests of God had become priests of Satan. Oh, terrible spectacle! And then that uproar, those cries of the populace! And lastly, Jesus, the Son of God, the Son of Man, Mary's own Son, disfigured and maltreated, fettered and covered with blows, driven along by the executioners, tottering rather than walking, jerked forward by the barbarous executioners who held the ropes that bound Him, and overwhelmed by a storm of mockery and malediction! Ah! Had He not been the most wretched, the most miserable in that tempest of Hell unchained, had He not been the only one calm and in loving prayer, Mary would never have known Him, so terribly was He disfigured. He had, besides, only His undergarment on, and that had been covered with dirt by the malicious executioners. As He approached her, she lamented as any Mother might have done: "Alas! Is this my Son? Ah! Is this my Son! O Jesus, my Jesus!" The procession hurried by. Jesus cast upon His Mother a side glance full of emotion. She became unconscious of all around, and John and Magdalen bore her away. But scarcely had she somewhat recovered herself when she requested John to accompany her again to

Pilate's palace.   (Vol. 4, pp. 177-178)

---

76. The Way of the Cross

Jesus is brought before Pilate, whose loathing
for the Jewish priests increases when he sees Jesus
so shockingly abused. He treats them with contempt
and scorn, but they lay before him the charges.
He interviews Jesus himself and finds no guilt in Him.
On hearing from the crowd that Jesus is from
Galilee, he sends Him to be judged by Herod.

The Blessed Virgin, standing with Magdalen and John
in a corner of the forum hall, had with unspeakable pain
beheld the whole of the dreadful scene just described, had
heard the clamorous shouts and cries. And now when
Jesus was taken to Herod, she begged to be conducted by
John and Magdalen back over the whole way of suffering
trodden by her Divine Son since His arrest the preceding
evening. They went over the whole route—to the judgment hall of Caiaphas, to the palace of Annas, and thence
through Ophel to Gethsemani on Mount Olivet. On many
places where Jesus had suffered outrage and injury, they
paused in heartfelt grief and compassion, and wherever
He had fallen to the ground the Blessed Mother fell on her
knees and kissed the earth. Magdalen wrung her hands,
while John in tears assisted the afflicted Mother to rise,
and led her on further. This was the origin of that devotion
of the Church, the Holy Way of the Cross, the origin of that
sympathetic meditation upon the bitter Passion of our
Divine Redeemer even before it was fully accomplished by
Him. Even then, when Jesus was traversing that most
painful way of suffering, did His pure and immaculate
Mother, in her undying, holy love, seek to share the
inward and outward pains of her Son and her God, vener-

ate and weep over His footsteps as He went to die for us, and offer all to the Heavenly Father for the salvation of the world.   (Vol. 4, p. 189)

77. Magdalen Understands Her Part in Jesus' Sufferings

Magdalen in her grief was like an insane person. Immeasurable as her love was her repentance. When, in her love, she longed to pour out her soul at the feet of Jesus as once the precious balm upon His head, full of horror she descried between her and the Redeemer the abyss of her crimes; then was the pain of repentance in all its bitterness renewed in her heart. When, in her gratitude, she longed to send up like a cloud of incense her thanksgiving for forgiveness received, she saw Him, full of pains and torments, led to death. With unspeakable grief, she comprehended that Jesus was undergoing all this on account of her sins, which He had taken upon Himself in order to atone for them with His own Blood. This thought plunged her deeper and deeper into an abyss of repentant sorrow. Her soul was, as it were, dissolved in gratitude and love, in sorrow and bitterness, in sadness and lamentation, for she saw and felt the ingratitude, the capital crime of her nation, in delivering its Saviour to the ignominious death of the cross. All this was expressed in her whole appearance, in her words and gestures.

John suffered and loved not less than Magdalen, but the untroubled innocence of his pure heart lent a higher degree of peace to his soul. . . .

During the dispersion of the disciples and the Passion of the Lord, Martha had a heavy duty to fulfill and she still discharged it. Though torn with grief, she had to see to everything, to lend a helping hand everywhere. She had to feed the dispersed and wandering, attend to their wants, provide nourishment for all. Her assistant in all this, as well as in the cooking, was Johanna Chusa, a widow whose husband had been a servant of Herod.

(Vol. 4, pp. 191, 388)

---

78. The Blessed Virgin and Magdalen Wipe up The Precious Blood after the Scourging

As Jesus is being taken to Herod, Pilate goes to his wife Claudia Procla, who tells him of the dreams she has had during the night. She begs him not to injure Jesus, as He is a great prophet. Pilate gives her his word that he will not condemn Jesus. Herod also finds Jesus innocent and sends Him back to Pilate. Looking for a way to release Jesus, Pilate offers to the crowd the choice of Jesus or Barabbas to be freed on the Pasch. The crowd chooses Barabbas. Pilate, still hoping to be able to free Jesus, orders Him to be scourged. Jesus is beaten and torn with whips and metal hooks for a full three-quarters of an hour and is then led away to be crowned with thorns.

Mary saw her lacerated Son driven past her by the executioners. With His garment He wiped the blood from His eyes in order to see His Mother. She raised her hands in agony toward Him and gazed upon His blood-stained footprints. Then, as the mob moved over to another side, I saw the Blessed Virgin and Magdalen approaching the place of scourging. Surrounded and hidden by the other holy women and some well-disposed people standing by, they cast themselves on their knees and soaked up the sacred Blood of Jesus with the linens until not a trace of it could be found.   (Vol. 4, p. 212)

79. Magdalen's Appearance

Magdalen . . . was tall, both in figure and carriage. . . . Her beauty, however, was now destroyed, owing to her violent repentance and intense grief. She was, if not decidedly ugly, at least painful to look upon, on account of the unrestrained fury of her passions. Her garments, wet and stained with mud, hung torn and disordered around her; her long hair floated loose and dishevelled under her wet, tossed veil. She was perfectly changed in appearance. She thought of nothing but her grief, and looked almost like one bereft of sense. There were many people here from Magdalum and the surrounding country who had known her in her early splendor, who had seen her in her wasting life of sin, and who had lost sight of her in her long retirement. Now they pointed her out with the finger and mocked at her forlorn appearance. Yes, there were some from Magdalum base enough even to throw mud at her as she passed along. But she did not notice it, so absorbed was she in her own sorrow.   (Vol. 4, pp. 222-223)

80. Mary and the Holy Women Go to Golgotha

Jesus is crowned with thorns, wrapped in an old military mantle, and a reed is placed in His hand. He is led back to Pilate, who has been trying to convince the crowd of Jesus' innocence. He presents Jesus to them with the words: "Behold the Man!" But they, being incited by the Pharisees, scream: "Crucify him!" Pilate again assures them that he finds no guilt in Him, but the mob continues to shout for His crucifixion. Pilate, realizing that he cannot reason with this raging multitude, washes his hands before them,

saying: "I am innocent of the blood of this just Man.
Look ye to it!" And rising up from the mob in one voice
comes the cry: "His Blood be upon us and upon our
children!" Thus Pilate, breaking his pledge to his wife,
pronounces the sentence of death and Jesus, embracing
His cross, begins the journey to Mount Golgotha.
Mary, John and Magdalen see the procession coming
toward them. As Jesus is passing, He falls. His Blessed
Mother rushes to Him and holds Him in her arms
for the last time. Being obliged by the soldiers to depart,
she is led away by John and the holy women.

After that most painful meeting with her Divine Son
carrying His cross before the dwelling of Caiaphas, the
most afflicted Mother was conducted by John and the holy
women, Johanna Chusa, Susanna, and Salome, to the
house of Nazareth in the vicinity of the corner gate. Here
the other holy women, in tears and lamentations, were
gathered around Magdalen and Martha. Some children
were with them. They now went all together, in number
seventeen, with the Blessed Virgin, careless of the jeers of
the mob, grave and resolute, and by their tears awe-
inspiring, across the forum, where they kissed the spot
upon which Jesus had taken up the burden of the cross.
Thence they proceeded along the whole of the sorrowful
way trodden by Him and venerated the places marked by
special sufferings. The Blessed Virgin saw and recognized
the footprints of her Divine Son, she numbered His steps,
pointed out to the holy women all the places consecrated
by His sufferings, regulated their halting and going forward on this Way of the Cross, which with all its details
was deeply imprinted in her soul.

The sufferings of the most afflicted Mother of Sorrows
on this journey, at the sight of the place of execution and
her ascent to it, cannot be expressed. They were twofold:
the pains of Jesus suffered interiorly and the sense of

being left behind. Magdalen was perfectly distracted, intoxicated and reeling, as it were, with grief, precipitated from agony to agony. From silence long maintained she fell to lamenting, from listlessness to wringing her hands, from moaning to threatening the authors of her misery. She had to be continually supported, protected, admonished to silence, and concealed by the other women.

They went up the hill by the gently sloping western side and stood in three groups, one behind the other, outside the wall enclosing the circle. The Mother of Jesus, her niece Mary Cleophas, Salome, and John stood close to the circle. Martha, Mary Heli, Veronica, Johanna Chusa, Susanna, and Mary Marcus stood a little distance back around Magdalen, who could no longer restrain herself. Still farther back were about seven others, and between these groups were some well-disposed individuals who carried messages backward and forward. The mounted Pharisees were stationed in groups at various points around the circle, and the five entrances were guarded by Roman soldiers.   (Vol. 4, pp. 262-264)

81. The Crucifixion

Jesus, being pulled from side to side by the cords tied about His waist, falls many times and is finally helped by Simon of Cyrene. Veronica offers her veil to Jesus, who gratefully accepts and, pressing it to His face, imprints His image upon it. The procession reaches the place of execution, and Jesus is again stripped of His clothing, reopening many of His wounds.

Jesus was now stretched on the cross by the executioners. He had lain Himself upon, it but they pushed Him lower down into the hollow places, rudely drew His right hand to the hole for the nail in the right arm of the cross, and tied His wrist fast. One knelt on His sacred breast and held the closing hand flat; another placed the long, thick nail, which had been filed to a sharp point, upon the palm of His sacred hand, and struck furious blows with the iron hammer. A sweet, clear, spasmodic cry of anguish broke from the Lord's lips, and His blood spurted out upon the arms of the executioners. The muscles and ligaments of the hand had been torn and, by the three-edged nail, driven into the narrow hole. I counted the strokes of the hammer, but my anguish made me forget their number. The Blessed Virgin sobbed in a low voice, but Magdalen was perfectly crazed.

The Blessed Virgin endured all this torture with Jesus. She was pale as a corpse, and low moans of agony sounded from her lips. The Pharisees were mocking and jesting at the side of the low wall by which she was standing; therefore, John led her to the other holy women at a still greater distance from the circle. Magdalen was like one out of her mind. She tore her face with her fingernails, till her eyes and cheeks were covered with blood.

(Vol. 4, pp. 268-270).

82. The Scribes and Pharisees on Mount Golgotha

Jesus' other hand is stretched into position and fastened
with the second nail. Both arms are tightly bound
to the cross to prevent the nails from ripping through
His hands. His feet are crossed, and the third nail
is hammered through both of them. The cross is
raised and dropped into the hole prepared for it.
The two thieves are crucified on either side of Jesus.
The slaughter of the Paschal lambs has begun.
The soldiers cast lots for Jesus' clothing.

After the crucifixion of the thieves and the distribution of the Lord's garments, the executioners gathered up their tools, addressed some mocking and insulting words to Jesus, and went their way. The Pharisees still present spurred up their horses, rode around the circle in front of Jesus, outraged Him in many abusive words, and then rode off. The hundred Roman soldiers with their commander also descended the mount and left the neighborhood, for fifty others had come up to take their place. The captain of this new detachment was Abenadar, an Arab by birth, who was later on baptized at Ctesiphon. The subaltern officer was Cassius. He was a kind of petty agent of Pilate, and at a subsequent period he received the name of Longinus. Twelve Pharisees, twelve Sadducees, twelve Scribes, and some of the Ancients likewise rode up the mount. Among the last-named were those Jews that had in vain requested of Pilate another inscription for the title of the cross. They were furious, for Pilate would not allow them even to appear in his presence. They rode around the circle and drove away the Blessed Virgin, calling her a dissolute woman. John took her to the women who were standing back. Magdalen and Martha supported her in their arms.   (Vol. 4, p. 281)

---

83. At the Foot of the Cross

The Pharisees mock Jesus and are joined in their insults by some of the soldiers and by Gesmas, the thief who is crucified on His left side, but Dismas defends Him and begs forgiveness of Him for the evil life he has led. Jesus blesses Dismas, saying: "Amen, I say to thee, this day thou shalt be with Me in Paradise!"

The Mother of Jesus, Mary Cleophas, Mary Magdalen, and John were standing around Jesus' cross, between it and those of the thieves, and looking up at the Lord. The Blessed Virgin, overcome by maternal love, was in her heart fervently imploring Jesus to let her die with Him. At that moment, the Lord cast an earnest and compassionate glance down upon His Mother and, turning His eyes toward John, said to her: "Woman, behold, this is thy son! He will be thy son more truly than if thou hadst given him birth." Then He praised John, and said: "He has always been innocent and full of simple faith. He was never scandalized, excepting when his mother wanted to have him elevated to a high position." To John, He said: "Behold, this is thy Mother!" and John reverently and like a filial son embraced beneath the cross of the dying Redeemer Jesus' Mother, who had now become his Mother also. After this solemn bequest of her dying Son, the Blessed Virgin was so deeply affected by her own sorrow and the gravity of the scene that the holy women, supporting her in their arms, seated her for a few moments on the earthen rampart opposite the cross, and then took her away from the circle to the rest of the holy women.   (Vol. 4, pp. 284-285)

---

84. "My God! My God! Why Hast Thou Forsaken Me!"

The sun is darkened, and fear fills Jerusalem.
Many utter lamentations, striking their breasts.
The High Priests light the lamps in the Temple,
trying to maintain order. The darkness increases.
Many of the lookers-on on Mount Golgotha flee back
to the city. A dense vapor hangs over everything,
and Jesus endures the pain of utter abandonment
by God the Father, experiencing for a time that
which is endured by a soul who has lost God forever.

Toward the third hour, Jesus cried in a loud voice; "Eli,

Eli, lamma sabacthani!" which means: "My God! My God! Why hast Thou forsaken Me!"

When this clear cry of Our Lord broke the fearful stillness around the cross, the scoffers turned toward it and one said: "He is calling Elias"; and another: "Let us see whether Elias will come to deliver Him." When the most afflicted Mother heard the voice of her Son, she could no longer restrain herself. She again pressed forward to the cross, followed by John, Mary Cleophas, Magdalen, and Salome.   (Vol. 4, p. 290)

---

85. "It Is Consummated!"

Loud murmurs and cries of grief resound everywhere.
The Pharisees, disheartened and fearing
an uprising, persuade the Centurion to close the
gate between the city and the place of execution.
The sky brightens, and Jesus, now perfectly
exhausted, utters the words: "I thirst." Abenadar,
the Centurion, places a sponge soaked with vinegar
on the tip of his lance and lifts it up to Jesus.

The hour of the Lord was now come. He was struggling with death, and a cold sweat burst out on every limb. John was standing by the cross and wiping Jesus' feet with his handkerchief. Magdalen, utterly crushed with grief, was leaning at the back of the cross. The Blessed Virgin, supported in the arms of Mary Cleophas and Salome, was standing between Jesus and the cross of the good thief, her gaze fixed upon her dying Son. Jesus spoke: "It is consummated!" And raising His head, He cried with a loud voice: "Father, into Thy hands I commend My Spirit!" The sweet, loud cry rang through Heaven and earth. Then he bowed His head and gave up the ghost. I saw His soul like a luminous phantom descending through the earth near the cross down to the sphere of Limbo. John and the holy women sank, face downward, prostrate on the earth. . . . When Jesus' hands became stiff, His Mother's eyes grew dim, the paleness of death overspread her countenance, her feet tottered, and she sank to the earth. Magdalen, John, and the others, yielding to their grief, fell also with veiled faces.   (Vol. 4, pp. 294, 297)

---

86. Jesus Is Pierced with the Lance

At the moment of Christ's death, there are great earthquakes all over the world, and terror falls upon all. The veil of the Temple is rent in two, and the dead rise from their graves to walk through Jerusalem, bearing witness to Jesus' divinity. Many of Jesus' tormentors are converted. The Pharisees ask Pilate for permission to break the legs of those crucified, that their bodies might be removed before the Sabbath. Joseph of Arimathea requests of Pilate the body of Jesus and makes the necessary arrangements for the burial. Jesus' soul descends into Limbo.

Meanwhile all was silent and mournful on Golgotha. The crowd had timidly dispersed to their homes. The Mother of Jesus, John, Magdalen, Mary Cleophas, and Salome were standing or sitting with veiled hands and in deep sadness opposite the cross. Some soldiers were seated on the earthen wall, their spears stuck in the ground near them. Cassius was riding around, and the soldiers were interchanging words with their companions posted at some distance below. The sky was lowering; all nature appeared to be in mourning. Things were in this position when six executioners were seen ascending the mount with ladders, spades, ropes, and heavy, triangular iron bars used for breaking the bones of malefactors.

When they entered the circle, the friends of Jesus drew back a little. New fear seized upon the heart of the Blessed Virgin, lest the body of Jesus was to be still further outraged, for the executioners mounted up the cross, roughly felt the sacred body, and declared that He was pretending to be dead. Although they felt that He was quite cold and stiff, yet they were not convinced that He was already dead. John, at the entreaty of the Blessed Virgin, turned to the soldiers, to draw them off for a while from the body of the Lord. The executioners next mounted the ladders of the crosses of the thieves. Two of them with their sharp clubs broke the bones of their arms above and below the elbows, while a third did the same above the knees and ankles. Gesmas roared frightfully, consequently the executioner finished him by three blows of the club on the breast. Dismas moaned feebly, and expired under the torture. He was the first mortal to look again upon his Redeemer. The executioners untwisted the cords, and allowed the bodies to fall heavily to the earth. Then tying ropes around them, they dragged them down into the valley between the mount and the city wall, and there buried them.

The executioners appeared still to have some doubts as to the death of the Lord, and His friends, after witnessing the terrible scene just described, were more anxious than ever for them to withdraw. Cassius, the subaltern officer, afterward known as Longinus, a somewhat hasty, impetuous man of twenty-five, whose airs of importance and officiousness joined to his weak, squinting eyes often exposed him to the ridicule of his inferiors, was suddenly seized by wonderful ardor. The barbarity, the base fury of the executioners, the anguish of the Blessed Virgin, and the grace accorded him in that sudden and supernatural impulse of zeal, all combined to make of him the fulfiller of a

Prophecy. His lance, which was shortened by having one section run into another, he drew out to its full length, stuck the point upon it, turned his horse's head, and drove him boldly up to the narrow space on top of the eminence upon which the cross was planted. There was scarcely room for the animal to turn, and I saw Cassius reigning him up in front of the chasm made by the cleft rock. He halted between Jesus' cross and that of the good thief, on the right of Our Saviour's body, grasped the lance with both hands, and drove it upward with such violence into the hollow, distended right side of the Sacred Body, through the entrails and the heart, that its point opened a little wound in the left breast. When with all his force he drew the blessed lance from the wide wound it had made in the right side of Jesus, a copious stream of blood and water rushed forth and flowed over his up-raised face, bedewing him with grace and salvation. He sprang quickly from his horse, fell upon his knees, struck his breast, and before all present proclaimed aloud his belief in Jesus.

Cassius was entirely changed, deeply touched and humbled. He had received perfect sight. The soldiers pres-ent, touched also by the miracle they had witnessed, fell on their knees, striking their breast and confessing Jesus, from the wide opening of whose right side blood and water were copiously streaming. It fell upon the clean stone, and lay there foaming and bubbling. The friends of Jesus gathered it up with loving care, Mary and Magdalen mingling with it their tears. The executioners, who meanwhile had received Pilate's order not to touch the body of Jesus, as he had given it to Joseph of Arimathea for burial, did not return.   (Vol. 4, pp. 312-315)

87. Jesus Is Taken Down from the Cross

*All is quiet in Jerusalem. Fear and anxiety keep the
inhabitants in their homes. Joseph of Arimathea
arrives at Mount Golgotha bringing, with his
servants, aromatic herbs, ointments and other supplies
needed for the embalming of Jesus' body.
When Abenadar returns, they begin the removal
of the Sacred Body from the cross. The nails
are removed, and Jesus' body, supported by the bands
of linen held by Joseph of Arimathea and Nicodemus,
is lowered into the arms of Abenadar. Cassius picks
up the three nails and lays them by the Blessed Virgin.*

The most holy Virgin and Magdalen were seated upon
the right side of the little mound between the cross of Dismas and that of Jesus. The other women were busied
arranging the spices and linens, the water, the sponges,
and the vessels. Cassius also drew near when he saw
Abenadar approaching, and imparted to him the miracle
wrought on his eyes. All were extremely touched. Their
movements were marked by an air of solemn sadness and
gravity. They worked with hearts full of love, but without
many words. Sometimes the silence in which the sacred
duties were quickly and carefully being rendered was broken by a deep sigh or a vehement exclamation of woe.
Magdalen gave way unrestrainedly to her grief. Her emotion was violent. No consideration, not even the presence
of so many around her, could make her repress it.

This taking down of Jesus from the Cross was inexpressibly touching. Everything was done with so much
precaution, so much tenderness, as if fearing to cause the
Lord pain. Those engaged in it were penetrated with all
the love and reverence for the Sacred Body that they had
felt for the Holy of Holies during His life. All were looking

up with eyes riveted, and accompanying every movement with raising of hands, tears, and gestures of pain and grief. But no word was uttered. When the men engaged in the sacred task gave expression to their reverent emotion, it was as if involuntary, as if they were performing some solemn function; and when necessary to communicate directions to one another, they did it in few words and a low tone. When the blows of the hammer by which the nails were driven out resounded, Mary and Magdalen, as well as all that had been present at the Crucifixion, were pierced with fresh grief, for the sound reminded them of that most cruel nailing of Jesus to the cross. They shuddered, as if expecting again to hear His piercing cries, and grieved anew over His death, proclaimed by the silence of those blessed lips. As soon as the Sacred Body was taken down, the men wrapped it in linen from the knees to the waist, and laid it on a sheet in His Mother's arms which, in anguish of heart and ardent longing, were stretched out to receive it.   (Vol. 4, pp. 324, 326)

88. Mary Receives Jesus into Her Arms

The Blessed Virgin was seated upon a large cover spread upon the ground, her right knee raised a little, and her back supported by a kind of cushion, made perhaps of mantles rolled together. There sat the poor Mother, exhausted by grief and fatigue, in the position best suited for rendering love's last, sad duties to the remains of her murdered Son. The men laid the Sacred Body on a sheet spread upon the Mother's lap. The adorable head of Jesus rested upon her slightly raised knee, and His body lay outstretched upon the sheet. Love and grief in equal degrees struggled in the breast of the Blessed Mother. She held in her arms the body of her beloved Son, whose long martyrdom she had been able to soothe by no loving ministrations; and at the same time she beheld the frightful maltreatment exercised upon it; she gazed upon its wounds now close under her eyes. She pressed her lips to His blood-stained cheeks, while Magdalen knelt with her face bowed upon His feet.

(Vol. 4, pp. 326-327)

89. The Blessed Mother and Magdalen Cleanse the Wounds of Jesus

The face of the Lord was hardly recognizable, so greatly was it disfigured by blood and wounds. The torn hair of the head and beard was clotted with blood. Mary washed the head and face and soaked the dried blood from the hair with sponges. As the washing proceeded, the awful cruelties to which Jesus had been subjected became more apparent, and roused emotions of compassion, sorrow, and tenderness as she went from wound to wound. With a sponge and a little linen over the fingers of her right hand, she washed the blood from the wounds of the head, from the broken eyes, the nostrils, and the ears. With the little piece of linen on the forefinger, she purified the half-opened mouth, the tongue, the teeth, and the lips. She divided into three parts the little that remained of His hair. One part fell on either side of the head, and the third over the back. The front hair, after disengaging and cleansing it, she smoothed behind His ears. When the sacred head had been thoroughly cleansed, the Blessed Virgin kissed the cheeks and covered it. Her care was next directed to the neck, the shoulders, the breast, and the back of the Sacred Body, the arms and the torn hands filled with blood. Ah, then was the terrible condition to which it had been reduced displayed in all its horror! The

bones of the breast, as well as all the nerves, were dislo-
cated and strained and thereby become stiff and inflexi-
ble. The shoulder upon which Jesus had borne the heavy
cross was so lacerated that it had become one great
wound, and the whole of the upper part of the body was
full of welts and cuts from the scourges. There was a small
wound in the left breast where the point of Cassius' lance
had come out, and in the right side was opened that great,
wide wound made by the lance, which had pierced His
heart through and through. Mary washed and purified all
these wounds, while Magdalen, kneeling before her, frequently lent assistance, though for the most part she
remained at Jesus' feet, bathing them for the last time,
more with her tears than with water, and wiping them
with her hair.

The head, the upper part of the body, and the feet of the
Lord had now been cleansed from blood. The Sacred Body
still lay in Mary's lap, bluish white, glistening like flesh
drained of blood, with here and there brown stains of
coagulated blood that looked like red moles, and red
places where the skin had been torn off. The Blessed Virgin covered the parts as they were washed, and began to
embalm the wounds, commencing with those of the head.
The holy women knelt by her in turn, presenting to her a
box from which, with the forefinger and thumb of the right
hand, she took out something like salve, or precious ointment, with which she filled and anointed all the wounds.
She put some upon the hair also, and I saw her taking the
hands of Jesus in her own left hand, reverently kissing
them, and then filling the wide wounds made by the nails
with the ointment, or sweet spices. The ears, nostrils, and
wound of Jesus' side she likewise filled with the same.
Magdalen was busied principally with the feet of Jesus.
She repeatedly wiped and anointed them, but only to
bedew them again with her tears, and she often knelt long

with her face pressed upon them.

(Vol. 4, pp. 328-330)

---

90. The Holy Women and Others Help Prepare for the Burial

The holy women helped in various ways, presenting when necessary vessels of water, sponges, towels, ointments and spices. When not so engaged, they remained at a little distance, attentively watching what was going on. Among them were Mary Cleophas, Salome, and Veronica, but Magdalen was always busied around the Sacred Body. Mary Heli, the Blessed Virgin's elder sister, and who was already an aged matron, was sitting apart on the earthwall of the circle, silently looking on. John lent constant assistance to the Blessed Virgin. He went to and fro between the women and the men, now helping the former in their task of love, and afterward assisting the latter in every way to prepare all things for the burial. Everything was thought of. The women had leathern water bottles, which they opened, and pressed the sides together to pour out their contents, also a vessel nearby on burning coals. They gave Mary and Magdalen clear water and fresh sponges according as required, squeezing into leathern bottles those that had been used. I think the round lumps that I saw them squeezing out must have been sponges.

The men meanwhile had retired to a little cave that lay deep on the southwestern side of the mount. There they completed their preparations for the burial and set all things in order. Cassius and a number of soldiers who had been converted to the Lord remained standing at a respectful distance. All the ill-disposed had returned to the city, and those now present served as a guard to prevent the approach of anyone likely to interrupt the last honors being shown to Jesus. Some of them, when called upon, rendered assistance here and there by handing different articles.   (Vol. 4, pp. 327-328)

---

91. The Body of Jesus Is Prepared for Burial

When the Blessed Virgin had anointed all the wounds, she bound up the sacred head in linen, but the covering for the face, attached to that of the head, she did not as yet draw down. With a gentle pressure, she closed the half-broken eyes of Jesus, and kept her hand upon them for a little while. Then she closed the mouth, embraced the Sacred Body of her Son, and weeping bitter tears, allowed her face to rest upon His. Magdalen's reverence for Jesus did not permit her to approach her face to His. She pressed it to His feet only.

Joseph and Nicodemus had already been standing awhile at some distance waiting when John drew near the Blessed Virgin with the request that she would permit them to take the body of Jesus, that they might proceed in their preparations for the burial, as the Sabbath was near. Once more Mary closely embraced Jesus, and in touching words, took leave of Him. The men raised the Most Sacred Body in the sheet upon which it was resting in the lap of His Mother, and carried it down to the place where the burial preparations were to be made. Mary's grief, which had been somewhat assuaged by her loving ministrations to Jesus, now burst forth anew, and quite overcome, she rested with covered head in the arms of the women. Magdalen, as if fearing that they wanted to rob her of her Beloved, with outstretched hands ran some steps after the Sacred Body, but soon she turned back again to the Blessed Virgin.

They carried the body of Jesus a little distance down

from Calvary's summit to a cave on the side of the mount
in which there was a beautiful flat rock. It was here that
the men had prepared the place for embalming. I saw first
a linen cloth, openworked something like a net. It looked
as if it had been pierced with a sharp instrument and was
like the large so-called hunger cloth (*Hungertuch*) that is
hung up in our churches during Lent. When as a child I
saw that cloth hanging up, I used to think it was the same
that I had seen at the preparations for the Lord's burial.
Perhaps it was pierced like a net in order to allow the
water used in washing to flow through it. I saw another
large cloth opened out. They laid the body of the Lord on
the openworked one, and some of them held the other over
it. Nicodemus and Joseph knelt down and, under cover of
this upper cloth, loosened from the lower part of Jesus'
body the bandage that they had bound around it from the
knees to the hips when taken down from the cross. They
removed likewise that other covering which Jonadab, the
nephew of His foster father Joseph, had given Him before
the Crucifixion. Thus with great regard to modesty, they
sponged, under cover of the sheet held over it, the lower
part of the Lord's body. Then, linen bands being stretched
under the upper part of the Sacred Body and the knees, it
was raised, still under cover of the sheet, and the back
treated in the same way without turning the body over.
They washed it until the water squeezed from the sponges
ran clean and clear. After that they poured water of myrrh
over the whole body, and I saw them laying it down and
reverently with their hands stretching it out at full
length, for it had stiffened in the position in which, when
in death it had sunk down upon the cross, the knees bent.
Under the hips they laid a linen strip, one ell in width and
about three in length, almost filled the lap with bunches
of herbs and fine, crisp threadlike plants, like saffron, and
then sprinkled over all a powder, which Nicodemus had

brought with him in a box. The bunches of herbs were
such as I have often seen on the celestial tables laid upon
little green and gold plates with blue rims. Next they
tightly bound the linen strip around the whole, drew the
end up between the sacred limbs, and stuck it under the
band that encircled the waist, thus fastening it securely.
After this they anointed the wounds of the thighs, scattered sweet spices over them, laid bunches of herbs
between the limbs all the way down to the feet, and bound
the whole in linen from the feet up.

John once more conducted the Blessed Virgin and the
other holy women to the sacred remains of Jesus. Mary
knelt down by Jesus' head, took a fine linen scarf that
hung around her neck under her mantle and which she
had received from Claudia Procla, Pilate's wife, and laid it
under the head of her Son. Then she and the other holy
women filled in the spaces between the shoulders and the
head, around the whole neck and up as far as the cheeks,
with herbs, some of those fine threadlike plants, and the
costly powder mentioned before, all of which the Blessed
Virgin bound up carefully in the fine linen scarf. Magdalen poured the entire contents of a little flask of precious balm into the wound of Jesus' side, while the holy
women placed aromatic herbs in the hands and all around
and under the feet. Then the men covered the pit of the
stomach and filled up the armpits and all other parts of
the body with sweet spices, crossed the stiffened arms
over the bosom, and closely wrapped the whole in the
large white sheet as far as the breast, just as a child is
swathed. Then having fastened under one of the armpits
the end of a broad linen band, they wound it round the
arms, the hands, the head, and down again around the
whole of the Sacred Body until it presented the appearance of a mummy. Lastly, they laid the Lord's body on the
large sheet, six ells long, that Joseph of Arimathea had

bought, and wrapped it closely around it. The Sacred Body was laid on it crosswise. Then one corner was drawn up from the feet to the breast, the opposite one was folded down over the head and shoulders, and the sides were doubled round the whole person.   (Vol. 4, pp. 330-333)

---

92. The Funeral Procession

The shroud with which Jesus' body was
wrapped is imprinted with His image.

The men now laid the Sacred Body on the leathern litter, placed over it a brown cover, and ran two poles along the sides. I thought right away of the Ark of the Covenant. Nicodemus and Joseph carried the front ends on their shoulders; Abenadar and John, the others. Then followed the Blessed Virgin, her elder sister Mary Heli, Magdalen, and Mary Cleophas; the group of women that had been seated at some distance, Veronica, Johanna Chusa, Mary Marcus; Salome, the wife of Zebedee; Mary Salome, Salome of Jerusalem, Susanna, and Anna, a niece of St. Joseph. She was the daughter of one of his brothers and had been reared in Jerusalem. Cassius and his soldiers closed the procession. The other women, namely, Maroni of Naim, Dina the Samaritan, and Mary the Suphanite were at the time with Martha and Lazarus in Bethania.

(Vol. 4, pp. 336-337)

---

93. Jesus Is Entombed

The holy women sat down upon a seat opposite the entrance of the grotto. The four men carried the Lord's body down into it, set it down, strewed the stone couch with sweet spices, spread over it a linen cloth, and deposited the sacred remains upon it. The cloth hung down over the couch. Then, having with tears and embraces given expression to their love for Jesus, they left the cave. The Blessed Virgin now went in, and I saw her sitting on the head of the tomb, which was about two feet from the ground. She was bending low over the corpse of her Child and weeping. When she left the cave, Magdalen hurried in with flowers and branches, which she had gathered in the garden and which she now scattered over the Sacred Body. She wrung her hands, and with tears and sighs embraced the feet of Jesus. When the men outside gave warning that it was time to close the doors, she went back to where the women were sitting. The men raised the cloth that was hanging over the side of the tomb, folded it around the Sacred Body, and then threw the brown cover over the whole. Lastly, they closed the brown doors, probably of copper or bronze, which had a perpendicular bar on the outside crossed by a transverse one. It looked like a cross. The great stone, intended for securing the doors and which was still lying outside the cave, was in shape almost like a chest or tomb, and was large enough for a man to lie at full length upon it. It was very heavy. By means of the poles brought from the garden entrance, the men rolled it into place before the closed doors of the tomb. The outside entrance was secured by a light door of wickerwork.

(Vol. 4, pp. 338-339)

94. The Return from the Burial

It was now the hour at which the Sabbath began. Nicodemus and Joseph returned to the city by a little private gate which, by special permission I think, Joseph had been allowed to make in the city wall near the garden.

They had previously informed the Blessed Virgin, Magdalen, John, and some of the women, who wanted to return to Mount Calvary to pray and to get some things they had left there, that this gate, as well as that of the Cenacle, would be opened to them whenever they would knock. Mary Heli, the Blessed Virgin's aged sister, was conducted back to the city by Mary Marcus and some other women. The servants of Nicodemus and Joseph went back to Mount Calvary for the tools and things they had left here.   (Vol. 4, pp. 339-340)

---

95. The Holy Women Prepare Herbs and Perfumes to Anoint the Body

Cassius returns to Jerusalem to relate to Pilate all the circumstances of Jesus' death and to request command of the guard to be placed before the sepulcher. Jesus' followers gather at the Cenacle, the bitter sorrow of all being renewed as each one tells his part. On Holy Saturday, Mary and the holy women visit the Temple, which has been very badly damaged by the earthquake. That evening they are met by Peter, James and John, who mourn with them. Mary consoles the holy women as they prepare the herbs and ointments for Jesus' body.

The table at which the holy women were standing had an upper support with crossed feet, something like a dresser, and it was covered with a cloth that hung down to the floor. I saw lying on it bunches of all kinds of herbs mixed and put in order, little flasks of ointment and nard water, and several flowers growing in pots, among which I remember one, a striped iris, or lily. The women packed them all in linen cloths. During Mary's absence, Magdalen, Mary Cleophas, Johanna Chusa, and Mary Salome went to the city to buy all these things. They wanted to go early next morning to scatter them over the body of Jesus in its winding sheet and pour upon it the perfumed water. I saw a part of it brought by the disciples from the dealer and left at the house without their going in to speak to the women.   (Vol. 4, p. 358)

---

96. Magdalen and the Holy Women Go to Anoint Jesus' Body

Cassius is in constant contemplation and prayer and has not left his post at the door of the sepulcher since he arrived late in the evening of Good Friday. Magdalen and the holy women finish preparing and packing the spices and are bidden by the Blessed Virgin to take some rest. The next morning, as they travel to the sepulcher, they anxiously inquire of one another: "Who will roll away for us the stone from the door?"

When the morning sky began to clear with a streak of white light, I saw Magdalen, Mary Cleophas, Johanna Chusa, and Salome, enveloped in mantles, leaving their abode near the Cenacle. They carried the spices packed in linen cloths, and one of them had a lighted lantern. They kept all hidden under their mantles. The spices consisted of fresh flowers for strewing over the Sacred Body, and also of expressed sap, essences, and oils for pouring over it. The holy women walked anxiously to the little gate belonging to Nicodemus. . . .

Salome had shared with Magdalen in defraying most of the cost. She was not the mother of John, but another Salome, a rich lady of Jerusalem, a relative of St. Joseph. At last the holy women concluded to set the spices on the stone before the tomb and to wait till some disciple would come who would open it for them. And so they went on toward the garden.   (Vol. 4, pp. 363, 365)

---

97. Magdalen at the Empty Tomb

*Jesus' soul re-enters His body. A warrior angel comes
down from Heaven, rolls the stone to one side and
seats himself upon it. The guards are stunned and
fall to the ground as if dead. Cassius recovers himself
quickly and, running into the tomb, feels the empty
linens. Full of wonder, he exits the tombs and waits.*

When, as they approached, the holy women noticed the
lanterns of the guard and the soldiers lying around, they
became frightened, and went a short distance past the
garden toward Golgatha. Magdalen, however, forgetful of
danger, hurried into the garden. Salome followed her at
some distance, and the other two waited outside.

Magdalen, seeing the guard, stepped back at first a few
steps toward Salome, then both made their way together
through the soldiers lying around and into the sepulcher.
They found the stone rolled away, but the doors closed,
probably by Cassius. Magdalen anxiously opened one of
them, peered in at the tomb, and saw the linens lying
empty and apart. The whole place was resplendent with
light, and an angel was sitting at the right of the tomb.
Magdalen was exceedingly troubled. She hurried out of
the garden of the sepulcher, off through the gate belonging
to Nicodemus, and back to the Apostles. Salome, too, who
only now entered the sepulcher, ran at once after Magdalen, rushed in fright to the women waiting outside the
garden, and told them of what had happened. Though
amazed and rejoiced at what they heard from Salome,
they could not resolve to enter the garden. It was not until
Cassius told them in a few words what he had seen, and
exhorted them to go see for themselves, that they took

courage to enter. Cassius was hurrying into the city to acquaint Pilate of all that had taken place. He went through the gate of execution. When with beating heart the women entered the sepulcher and drew near the holy tomb, they beheld standing before them the two angels of the tomb in priestly robes, white and shining. The women pressed close to one another in terror and, covering their faces with their hands, bowed trembling almost to the ground. One of the angels addressed them. They must not fear, he said, nor must they look for the Crucified here. He was alive, He had risen, He was no longer among the dead. Then the angel pointed out to them the empty tomb, and ordered them to tell the disciples what they had seen and heard, and that Jesus would go before them into Galilee. They should, continued the angel, remember what the Lord had said to them in Galilee, namely, "The Son of Man will be delivered into the hands of sinners. He will be crucified, and on the third day, He will rise again." The holy women, shaking and trembling with fear, though still full of joy, tearfully gazed at the tomb and the linens, and departed, taking the road toward the gate of execution. They were still very much frightened. They did not hurry, but paused from time to time and looked around from the distance, to see whether they might not possibly behold the Lord, or whether Magdalen was returning.

(Vol. 4, pp. 366-367)

98. Magdalen's Announcement To the Disciples

Meanwhile Magdalen reached the Cenacle like one beside herself, and knocked violently at the door. Some of the disciples were still asleep on their couches around the walls, while several others had risen and were talking together. Peter and John opened the door. Magdalen, without entering, merely uttered the words: "They have taken the Lord from the tomb! We know not where"—and ran back in great haste to the garden of the sepulcher. Peter and John followed her, but John outstripped Peter.

(Vol. 4, pp. 367)

99. The Risen Lord Appears to Magdalen

Magdalen was quite wet with dew when she again reached the garden and ran to the tomb. Her mantle had slipped from her head down on her shoulders, and her long hair had fallen around loose. As she was alone, she was afraid to enter the sepulcher at once, so she waited out on the step at the entrance. She stooped down, trying to see through the low doors into the cave and even as far as the stone couch. Her long hair fell forward as she stooped, and she was trying to keep it back with her hands when she saw the two angels in white priestly garments sitting at the head and the foot of the tomb, and heard the words: "Woman, why weepest thou?" She cried out in her grief: "They have taken my Lord away! I know not where they have laid Him!" Saying this and seeing nothing but the linens, she turned weeping, like one seeking something, and as if she must find Him. She had a dim presentiment that Jesus was near, and even the apparition of the angels could not turn her from her one idea. She did not appear conscious of the fact that it was an angel that spoke to her. She thought only of Jesus; her only thought was: "Jesus is not here! Where is Jesus?" I saw her running a few steps from the sepulcher and then returning like one half-distracted and in quest of something. Her long hair fell on her shoulders. Once she drew the whole mass on the right shoulder through both hands, then flung it back and gazed around. About ten steps from the sepulcher and toward the east, where the garden rose in the direction of the city, she spied in the gray light of dawn, standing among the bushes behind a palm tree, a figure clothed in a long white garment. Rushing toward it, she heard once more the words: "Woman, why weepest thou? Whom seekest thou?" She thought it was the gardener. I saw that he had a spade in his hand and on his head a flat hat, which had a piece of something like bark standing out in front, as a protection from the sun. It was just like that I had seen on the gardener in the parable which Jesus, shortly before His Passion, had related to the women in Bethania. The apparition was not resplendent. It looked like a person clad in long white garments and seen at twilight. At the words: "Whom seekest thou?" Magdalen at once answered: "Sir, if thou hast taken Him hence, show me where thou hast laid Him! I will take Him away!" And she again glanced around, as if to see whether he had not laid Him someplace near. Then Jesus, in His well-known voice, said: "Mary!" Recognizing the voice, and forgetting the crucifixion, death and burial, now that He was alive, she turned quickly and, as once before, exclaimed: "Rabboni!" (Master!). She fell on her knees before Him and stretched out her arms toward His feet. But Jesus raised His hand to keep her off, saying: "Do not touch Me, for I am not yet ascended to My Father. But go to My brethren, and say to them: I ascend to My Father and to your Father, to My God and to your God." At these words, the Lord vanished. It was explained to me why Jesus said: "Do not touch Me," but I have only an indistinct remembrance of it. I think He said it because Magdalen was so impetuous. She seemed possessed of the idea that Jesus was alive just as He was before, and that everything was as it used to be. Upon Jesus' words that He

had not yet, since His Resurrection, presented Himself to
His Heavenly Father, had not yet thanked Him for His
victory over death and for Redemption, I understood by
those words that the first fruits of joy belong to God. It
was as if Jesus had said that Magdalen should recollect
herself and thank God for the mystery of Redemption
just accomplished and His conquest over death. After the
disappearance of the Lord, Magdalen rose up quickly
and again, as if in a dream, ran to the tomb. She saw the
two angels, she saw the empty linens, and hurried, now
certain of the miracle, back to her companions.(Vol.   4,
pp. 367-369)

---

100. Peter and John See the Empty Tomb

It may have been about half-past three o'clock when
Jesus appeared to Magdalen. Scarcely had she left the
garden when John approached, followed by Peter. John
stood outside the entrance of the cave and stooped down
to look, through the outer doors of the sepulcher, at the
half-opened doors of the tomb, where he saw the linens
lying. Then came Peter. He stepped down into the sepulcher and went to the tomb, in the center of which he saw
the winding sheet lying. It was rolled together from both
sides toward the middle, and the spices were wrapped in
it. The bandages were folded around it, as women are
accustomed to roll together such linens when putting
them away. The linen that had covered the sacred face
was lying to the right next the wall. It too was folded.
John now followed Peter to the tomb, saw the same
things, and believed in the Resurrection. All that the
Lord had said, all that was written in the Scriptures, was
now clear to them. They had had only an imperfect com-
prehension of it before. Peter took the linens with him

under his mantle. Both again went back by the little gate belonging to Nicodemus, and John once more got ahead of Peter.

As long as the Sacred Body lay in the tomb, the two angels sat one at the head, the other at the foot, and when Magdalen and the two Apostles came, they were still there. It seems to me that Peter did not see them. I heard John afterward saying to the disciples of Emmaus that, on looking into the tomb, he saw one angel. Perhaps it was through humility that he forbore to mention it in his Gospel, that he might not appear to have seen more than Peter. . . .

Meanwhile, Magdalen had reached the holy women and told them of the Lord's apparition. Then she too hurried on to the city through the neighboring gate of the execution, but the others went again to the garden, outside of which Jesus appeared to them in a white flowing garment that concealed even His hands. He said: "All hail!" they trembled and fell at His feet. Jesus waved His hand in a certain direction while addressing to them some words, and vanished. The holy women then hastened through the Bethlehem gate on Sion, to tell the disciples in the Cenacle that they had seen the Lord and what He had said to them. But the disciples would not at first credit Magdalen's report, and, until the return of Peter and John, they looked upon the whole affair as the effect of women's imagination.

(Vol. 4, pp. 369-371)

101. Jesus Appears in the Hall
Of the Last Supper

The guards awake and, full of fear and confusion,
hurry back to the city. About an hour after the
Resurrection, Cassius goes to Pilate and relates
all that has happened. Four guards who tell the truth
are imprisoned; Jesus' enemies spread the report that
Jesus' body has been carried away by His disciples.
The Jews purify the Temple and continue the
interrupted Paschal solemnities. Annas becomes
as one possessed and must be confined for the
remainder of his life. Jesus appears at Emmaus.

On the evening of the same day, many of the disciples
and all the Apostles excepting Thomas assembled with
Nicodemus and Joseph of Arimathea in the hall of the
Last Supper, the doors being closed. They stood ranged in
a triple circle under the lamp that hung from the center of
the ceiling, and prayed. They seemed to be engaged in
some after-celebration of mourning or thanksgiving, for
the Paschal solemnities ended today in Jerusalem.

. . . The Blessed Virgin was, during the whole celebra-
tion, with Mary Cleophas and Magdalen in the hall outside, which opened into the supper room. Peter preached
at intervals during the prayers. . . .

And now I saw Peter going behind a screen, or hanging
tapestry, into a recess of the hall which one might fail to
remark, since the screen was like the entire wainscoting.
In the center of this recess, on the Paschal hearth, stood
the Blessed Sacrament. There was a side compartment
into which they had pushed the table, which was one foot
high, after they had eaten reclining around it under the
lamp. On this table stood a deep oval dish covered with a
little white cloth, which Peter took to the Lord. In the dish
were a piece of fish and some honey. Jesus gave thanks

and blessed the food, ate and gave a portion of it some, but not to all. To His Holy mother also and the other women, who were standing in the doorway of the outer hall, He likewise distributed some. After that I saw Him teaching and imparting strength. . . .

Jesus explained to the Apostles several points of Holy Scripture relative to Himself and the Blessed Sacrament, and ordered the Latter to be venerated at the close of the Sabbath solemnities. He spoke of the Sacred Mystery of the Ark of the Covenant; of the bones and relics of ancestors and their veneration, thus to obtain their intercession; of Abraham, and of the bones of Adam which he had had in his possession and which he had laid on the altar when offering sacrifice. . . . Jesus spoke too of the Mystery contained in the Ark of the Covenant. He said that that Mystery was now His Body and Blood, which He gave to them forever in the Sacrament. He spoke of His own Passion and of some wonderful things relating to David of which they were ignorant and which He explained. Lastly, He bade them go in a couple of days to the region of Sichar, and there proclaim His Resurrection. After that He vanished.   (Vol. 4, pp. 381-385)

102. Magdalen's Holy Courage

After Jesus appears to the Apostles in the hall
of the Last Supper they speak of this to Thomas;
but he, having been absent, cannot bring
himself to believe what they say of Him.
The Apostles now teach and cure publicly.

Magdalen, in her sorrow and love, was above all fear. She was perfectly heroic and without a thought of danger. She took no rest, but often left the house, hurried through the streets with streaming hair, and wherever she found listeners, whether in their homes or in public places, she accused them as the murderers of the Lord, vehemently recounting all they had done to the Saviour, and announcing to them His Resurrection. If she found no one to listen to her, she wandered through the gardens and told it to the flowers, the trees, and the fountains. Oftentimes a crowd gathered around her, some compassionating her, others insulting her on account of her past life. She was little esteemed by the crowd, for she had once given great scandal. I saw that her present violent conduct scandalized some of the Jews, and about five of them wanted to seize her, but she passed straight through them and went on as before. She had lost sight of the whole world, she sighed only after Jesus.   (Vol. 4, pp. 387-388)

---

103. Jesus Appears Again to the Apostles

*Jesus appears in many places, staying only for
a few moments and then vanishing. The Blessed Virgin
continues the devotion of the Holy Way of the Cross
that she had begun after the death of her Son.
The Apostles prepare to celebrate the second Agape.*

While these preparations were being made, I saw Thomas entering the Supper Room. He passed through the Apostles who were already robed, and put on his own long white garment. As he went along, I saw the Apostles accosting him. Some caught him by the sleeve, others gesticulated with the right hand as they spoke, as if emphatically protesting against him. But he behaved like one in a hurry to vest and as if he could not credit the account given him of the wonderful things which had happened in that place. While all this was going on, a man entered the hall. He appeared to be a servant. He wore an apron and had in one hand a little lighted lamp, in the other a rod terminating in a hook. With the latter he drew down the lamp that was suspended from the center of the ceiling, lighted it, and again pushed it up. Then he left the hall! And now I saw the Blessed Virgin, Magdalen, and another woman come into the house. The Blessed Virgin and Magdalen entered the hall, Peter and John going to meet them. The third woman remained in the antechamber. The entrance hall was opened into the Supper Room, also some of the side halls. The exterior doors leading into the courtyard, as well as those of the court itself, were shut. A great many disciples were gathered in the side halls.

As soon as Mary and Magdalen entered, the doors were closed and all ranged for prayer. The holy women remained reverently standing on either side of the door, their arms crossed upon their breast. The Apostles kneeling before the Holy of Holies, prayed again as before; then standing under the lamp, they sang Psalms, choir and choir. Peter stood before the lamp, his face toward the Holy of Holies, John and James the Less at his side. Right and left of the lamp were the other Apostles. The side toward the Holy of Holies was left free. Peter stood between the two, his back to the door, so that the two holy women were standing behind him at some distance.

After some time there was a pause in the assembly, an intermission of prayer, or as if prayer was at an end, and they began to speak of going to the Sea of Tiberius and of how they would disperse. But soon they assumed an expression of rapt attention, called up by the approach of the Lord. At the same moment, I saw Jesus in the courtyard. He was resplendent with light, clothed in white garments and a white girdle. He directed His steps to the door of the outer hall, which opened of itself before Him and closed behind Him. The disciples in the outer hall saw the door opening of itself, and fell back on both sides to

make room. But Jesus walked quickly through the hall
into the Supper Room and stepped between Peter and
John, who, like all the other Apostles, fell back on either
side.

Jesus did not enter walking properly so called, that is,
in the usual way of mortals, and yet it was not a floating
along, or hovering, as I have seen spirits doing. It
reminded me, as I saw them all falling back, of a priest in
his alb passing through a crowded congregation. Everything in the hall appeared to become suddenly large and
bright. Jesus was environed with light. The Apostles had
fallen back from the radiant circle; otherwise, they would
not have been able to seen Him.

Jesus' first words were: "Peace be to you!" Then He
spoke with Peter and John, and rebuked them for something. They had departed a little from His directions, in
order to follow their own ideas about something, and consequently they had not met with success. It related to
some of the cures they had sought to effect on their return
from Sichar and Thanath-Silo. They had not followed
Jesus' directions to the letter, and therefore had not been
entirely successful. They had done something according to
their own ideas. Jesus told them that, if it happened
again, they should act otherwise. Jesus now stepped
under the lamp, and the Apostles closed around Him . . .

When Jesus grasped Thomas' hand, I saw that His
wounds were not like bloody marks, but like little radiant suns. The other disciples were very greatly touched
by this scene. They leaned forward, without, however,
crowding, to see what the Lord was allowing Thomas
to feel. I saw the Blessed Virgin during the whole time
of Jesus' stay, perfectly motionless, as if absorbed in
calm, deep interior recollection. Magdalen appeared
more agitated, yet manifested far less emotion than did
the disciples. . . .

Jesus addressed neither His Blessed Mother nor Magdalen.   (Vol. 4, pp. 392-394, 396)

---

104. Agape in Bethania

Jesus remained with His Apostles in the Supper Room
for some time, explaining many mysteries to them.
He blessed Peter, investing him with chief
power over the others and filling his soul with
new strength and vigor. Peter addressed the assembly,
and as he was speaking, Jesus vanished.
Jesus appears to the Apostles at the Sea of Galilee
and tells Peter to feed His sheep. Peter gathers more
disciples. He teaches great crowds, inspiring many
to follow Jesus. He and the other Apostles and disciples
travel back to Bethania to establish the Community.

I saw the Apostles in Bethania, whither they were followed by about three hundred of the Faithful, among them fifty women. They had given over their goods to the Community. The Blessed Virgin also had come from Jerusalem to Bethania, and was stopping in Martha and Magdalen's house. There was a great Love Feast of bread-breaking and passing round of the cup held in the open hall of Lazarus' court.   (Vol. 4, p. 408)

---

105. The Community

Many places in Jerusalem where Jesus suffered
during His Passion or taught before His death have
been demolished or rendered unapproachable,
to prevent worship and veneration. The community
grows after each teaching, both men and women
giving all their earthly belongings to join.

Peter's wife and daughter, Mark's wife, and other women had come from Bethsaida to Bethania, where they dwelt under tents. They had no communication whatever with the men. They came into the presence of the Apostles only for instruction, and they employed themselves in weaving and twisting long strips of stuff and coarse covers for tents, many of them working at the same time upon one piece. The Blessed Virgin also, along with Martha and Magdalen, worked at embroidery, sometimes reclining, sometimes walking about, work in hand. I saw the Blessed Virgin embroidering in delicate colors, figures something like an Apostle, or the Lord Himself, on a yellow, brown, or sky-blue ground. The figures were not so enveloped in mantles as formerly. Once they embroidered a representation of the Most Holy Trinity. It was like God the Father handing the cross to the Son, who looked like a High Priest. From both proceeded the Holy Ghost, though not in the form of a dove, for instead of wings there were arms. The figures were arranged more in a triangular form than one below the other. I have seen in the earliest churches of that period vestments that Mary had embroidered.

Magdalen and Martha gave up their houses at Bethania to the new converts, and Lazarus delivered over all that he owned to the Community. Nicodemus and Joseph of Arimathea did the same. They assumed the charge of providing for the Community and distributing the alms. But when they were ordained priests, Peter appointed deacons in their place.   (Vol. 4, pp. 415-416, 418)

106. Before the Ascension

Jesus celebrates His last love feast on earth with the Apostles, disciples and holy women at the Cenacle on the night before His Ascension into Heaven.

The love feast over, all assembled outside the hall under the trees. Jesus addressed to them a long instruction, and ended by giving them His blessing. To His Blessed Mother, who was standing in front of the holy women, He extended His hand. All were very much affected, and I felt that Magdalen ardently longed to embrace Jesus' feet. But she restrained her desire, for His demeanor was so grave that He inspired holy fear. When He left them, they wept very much. It was not, however, an exterior weeping, it was like the weeping of the soul. I did not see the Blessed Virgin shedding tears. I never saw her actually weeping excepting when she lost Jesus, a Boy of twelve, on her return journey from the Paschal festival, and again when she stood under the cross after His death. The assembly broke up before midnight.

During the last days, Magdalen, Martha, and Mary Cleophas received the Blessed Sacrament.

(Vol. 4, pp. 421-422)

107. Before Peter's First Mass

*Jesus ascends to Heaven. Matthias is elected to replace
Judas in the apostolate. The Holy Spirit descends
upon the Blessed Virgin, the Apostles, the disciples,
and the holy women. Peter imposes hands upon
James the Less, Bartholomew, Matthias, Thomas and
Jude Thaddeus, who depart for the Pool of Bethsaida
to consecrate the water and administer Baptism.
The Apostles speak in tongues. The old synagogue near
the Pool of Bethsaida is now converted into a church,
where the community prepares for Peter's first Mass.*

Toward eight o'clock that morning, they left the Temple.
In the court of the heathens they formed in a long procession, two by two, first the Apostles, after them the disciples, then the baptized and the newly converted. They
proceeded across the cattle market to the sheep gate, out
into the Valley of Josaphat, and thence up Sion to the
house of the Last Supper. The Blessed Virgin and the
other women had left the Temple some time previously, in
order to kneel alone before the Blessed Sacrament and
pray. Magdalen prayed in the entrance hall, sometimes
standing, sometimes kneeling, or again prostrate on the
ground, her arms outstretched. The other women had
retired into their cells adjoining the church of Bethsaida.
There they dwelt two together, occupying their time in
washing and preparing the baptismal garments for the
neophytes, and with the arrangement of such things for
distribution.   (Vol. 4, pp. 439-440)

108. The Blessed Virgin Moves to Ephesus; Lazarus and His Sisters Set Out over the Sea

*Peter ordains many of the disciples. He celebrates
his first Mass, after which he and the other
Apostles perform many cures and other miracles.
Peter and John are arrested and released.*

About one year after the Crucifixion of Our Lord,
Stephen was stoned, though no further persecution of the
Apostles took place at that time. The rising settlement of
new converts around Jerusalem, however, was dissolved,
the Christians dispersed, and some were murdered. A few
years later, a new storm arose against them. Then it was
that the Blessed Virgin, who until that time had dwelt in
the small house near the Cenacle and in Bethania,
allowed herself to be conducted by John to the region of
Ephesus, where the Christians had already made settle-
ments. This happened a short time after the imprison-
ment of Lazarus and his sisters by the Jews and their
setting out over the sea.   (Vol. 4, p. 448)

---

109. The Death of the Blessed Virgin

*The Apostles disperse to teach of Jesus in far off
countries. The Blessed Virgin erects the stations of the
Holy Way of the Cross near her home in Ephesus.*

As the Blessed Virgin felt her end approaching, in
accordance with the directions of her Divine Son, she
called the Apostles to her by prayer. She was now in her
sixty-third year. At the time of Christ's birth, she was in
her fifteenth. Before His Ascension Jesus had made
known to His most holy Mother what she should say at
the end of her earthly career to the Apostles and some of
the disciples who should be with her. He told her also that

she should bless them, and that it would conduce very much to their welfare and eternal salvation. He entrusted to her also certain spiritual labors for the general good, which being accomplished, her longing after Heaven was to be realized. Jesus had at the same time made known to Magdalen that she was to live concealed in the wilderness and that Martha was to establish a community of women. He added that He Himself would always be with them.   (Vol. 4, pp. 458-459)

Three years after the Crucifixion all the Apostles met in Jerusalem, after which Peter and John left the city and Mary accompanied the latter to Ephesus. Then arose in Jerusalem the persecution against Lazarus, Martha, and Magdalen. The last-named had up to that time been doing penance in the desert, in the cave to which Elizabeth had escaped with John during the massacre of the Innocents. The Apostles, in that first reunion, brought together all that belonged to the body of the Church. When half of the time of Mary's life after Christ's Ascension had flown, about the sixth year after that event, the Apostles were again assembled in Jerusalem. It was then they drew up the Creed, made rules, relinquished all that they possessed, distributed it to the poor, and divided the Church into dioceses, after which they separated and went into far-off heathen countries. At Mary's death they all met again for the last time. When they again separated for distant countries, it was until death.   (Vol. 4, pp. 7-8)

APPENDIX I

A Relic of Magdalen's Clothing

From *The Life and Revelations of Anne Catherine Emmerich*, by Rev. Carl Schmöger, C.SS.R., Vol. 2, pp. 386-387.

Toward dusk that same day, the Pilgrim [Clemens Brentano] opened another of the little parcels on which were inscribed the words: *"From the clothing of a Saint,"* and which contained also a bone and a label. It was almost dark and the objects were so very small that he did not imagine Sister Emmerich noticed his action. To his surprise, she called to him: "Take care of that label! The relic shines; it is authentic!" He handed her the particle of bone, when she instantly fell into contemplation. On returning to herself she said: "I have been far away to Bethany, Jerusalem, and France. The bone belongs to Martha; the clothing to Magdalen. It is blue with yellow flowers and green leaves, the remnants of her vanity, which she wore under a mourning mantle, in Bethania, at the raising of Lazarus. This dress remained in Lazarus' house when he and his sisters went to France, and pious friends took it as a memento. Some pilgrims when visiting their tomb in France, wrapped this relic in a part of the dress, thinking both belonged to Magdalen; but only the clothing is hers, the relic is Martha's." When the Pilgrim closely examined the inscription, he indeed found: *"Sancta Maria Magdalen."*

APPENDIX II

Mary Magdalen and Martha in Scripture

The following paragraph is taken from St. Luke's Gospel.

"Now it came to pass as they went, that he entered a certain town: and a certain woman named Martha, received him into her house. And she had a sister called Mary, who sitting also at the Lord's feet, heard his word. But Martha was busy about much serving. Who stood and said: Lord, hast thou no care that my sister hath left me alone to serve? Speak to her therefore, that she help me. And the Lord answering, said to her: Martha, Martha, thou art careful, and art troubled about many things: But one thing is necessary. Mary hath chosen the best part, which shall not be taken away from her."

(*Luke* 10:38-42)

APPENDIX III

Mary Magdalen in Catholic Traditions

The following article, "Mary Magdalen," is from
The Catholic Encyclopedia, 1910, Vol. 9, p. 761.

Mary Magdalen, so called either from Magdala near
Tiberius, on the west shore of Galilee, or possibly from a
Talmudic expression meaning "curling women's hair,"
which the Talmud explains as of an adultress. In the New
Testament she is mentioned among the women who
accompanied Christ and ministered to Him (*Luke* 7:2-3),
where it is also said that seven devils had been cast out
of her. (*Mark* 16:9). She is next named as standing at the
foot of the Cross. (*Mark* 15:40; *Matt.* 27:56; *John* 19:25;
Luke 23:49). She saw Christ laid in the tomb, and she was
the first recorded witness of the Resurrection. The Greek
Fathers, as a whole, distinguish the three persons: the
"sinner" of *Luke* 7:36-50; the sister of Martha and
Lazarus (*Luke* 10:38-42; *John* 11); and Mary Magdalen.
On the other hand, most of the Latins hold that these
three were one and the same. Protestant critics, however,
believe there were two, if not three, distinct persons. It is
impossible to demonstrate the identity of the three; but
those commentators undoubtedly go too far who assert,
as does Westcott (on *John* 11:1), "that the identity of
Mary with Mary Magdalene is a mere conjecture supported by no direct evidence, and opposed to the general
tenor of the gospels." It is the identification of Mary of
Bethany with the "sinner" of *Luke* 7:37 which is most
combatted by Protestants. (See Plummer, *International
Critical Comment on St. Luke*, p. 209.) It almost seems as

143

if this reluctance to identify the "sinner" with the sister of Martha were due to a failure to grasp the full significance of the forgiveness of sin. (See Mayor in Hastings, *Dictionary of the Bible*, III, 284.) The harmonizing tendencies of so many modern critics, too, are responsible for much of the existing confusion.

The first fact mentioned in the Gospel relating to the question under discussion is the anointing of Christ's feet by a woman, a "sinner" in the city. (*Luke* 7:37-50). This belongs to the Galilean ministry, it precedes the miracle of the feeding of the five thousand and the third Passover. Immediately afterward St. Luke describes a missionary circuit in Galilee and tells us of the women who ministered to Christ, among them being "Mary who is called Magdalen, out of whom seven devils were gone forth" (*Luke* 8:2); but he does not tell us that she is to be identified with the "sinner" of the previous chapter. In *Luke* 10:38-42, he tells us of Christ's visit to Martha and Mary "in a certain town"; it is impossible to identify this town, but it is clear from *Luke* 9:53 that Christ had definitively left Galilee, and it is quite possible that this "town" was Bethany. This seems confirmed by the preceding parable of the good Samaritan, which must almost certainly have been spoken on the road between Jericho and Jerusalem. But here again we note that there is no suggestion of an identification of the three persons, viz., the "sinner," Mary Magdalen, and Mary of Bethany; and if we had only St. Luke to guide us we should certainly have no grounds for so identifying them. St. John, however, clearly identifies Mary of Bethany with the woman who anointed Christ's feet. (*Luke* 12; cf. *Matt.* 26; *Mark* 14). It is remarkable that already in *John* 11:2, St. John has spoken of Mary as "she that anointed the Lord's feet," ἡ ἀλείψασα. It is commonly said that he refers to the subsequent anointing which he himself describes in 12:3-8; but it may be questioned whether he would have used ἡ ἀλείψασα if another woman, and she a "sinner" in the city, had done the same. It is conceivable that St. John, just because he is writing so long after the event and at a time when Mary was dead, wishes to point out to us that she was really the same as the "sinner." In the same way St. Luke may have veiled her identity precisely because he did not wish to defame one who was yet living; he certainly does something similar in the case of St. Matthew, whose identity with Levi the publican (*Luke* 5:7) he conceals.

If the foregoing arguement holds good, Mary of Bethany and the "sinner" are one and the same. But an examination of St. John's Gospel makes it almost impossible to deny the identity of Mary of Bethany with Mary Magdalen. From St. John we learn the name of the "woman" who anointed Christ's feet previous to the last supper. We may remark here that it seems unnecessary to hold that because St. Matthew and St. Mark say "two days before the Passover," while St. John says "six days," there were, therefore, two distinct anointings following one another. St. John does not necessarily mean that the supper and the anointing took place six days before, but only that Christ came to Bethany six days before the Passover. At that supper, then, Mary received the glorious encomium, "she hath wrought a good work upon Me . . . in pouring this ointment upon My body she hath done it for My burial . . . wheresoever this Gospel shall be preached . . . that also which she hath done shall be told for a memory of her." Is it credible, in view of all this, that this Mary should have no place at the foot of the Cross, nor at the tomb of Christ? Yet it is Mary Magdalen who, according to all the Evangelists, stood at the foot of the Cross and assisted at the entombment and was the first recorded witness of the Resurrection. And while St. John calls her

"Mary Magdalen" in *John* 19:25, 20:1 and 18, he calls her simply "Mary" in *John* 20:11 and 16.

In the view we have advocated the series of events forms a consistent whole; the "sinner" comes early in the ministry to seek for pardon; she is described immediately afterwards as Mary Magdalen "out of whom seven devils were gone forth"; shortly after, we find her "sitting at the Lord's feet and hearing His words." To the Catholic mind it all seems fitting and natural. At a later period Mary and Martha turn to "the Christ, the Son of the Living God," and He restores to them their brother Lazarus; a short time afterward they make Him a supper and Mary once more repeats the act she had performed when a penitent. At the Passion she stands near by; she sees Him laid in the tomb; and she is the first witness of His Resurrection—excepting always His Mother, to whom He must needs have appeared first, though the New Testament is silent on this point. In our view, then, there were two anointings of Christ's feet—it should surely be no difficulty that St. Matthew and St. Mark speak of His head—the first (*Luke* 7), took place at a comparatively early date; the second, two days before the last Passover. But it was one and the same woman who performed this pious act on each occasion.

SUBSEQUENT HISTORY OF ST. MARY MAGDALEN

The Greek Church maintains that the saint retired to Ephesus with the Blessed Virgin and there died, that her relics were transferred to Constantinople in 886 and are there preserved. Gregory of Tours, *De miraculis*, I, xxx, supports the statement that she went to Ephesus. However, according to a French tradition (see LAZARUS OF BETHANY, SAINT), Mary, Lazarus, and some companions came to Marseilles and converted the whole of Provence. Magdalen is said to have retired to a hill, La Sainte-Baume, near by where she gave herself up to a life of penance for thirty years. When the time of her death arrived she was carried by angels to Aix and into the oratory of St. Maximinus, where she received the Viaticum; her body was then laid in an oratory constructed by St. Maximinus at Villa Lata, afterward called St. Maximin. History is silent about these relics till 745, when, according to the chronicler Sigebert, they were removed to Vézelay through fear of the Saracens. No record is preserved of their return, but in 1279, when Charles II, King of Naples, erected a convent at La Sainte-Baume for the Dominicans, the shrine was found intact, with an inscription stating why they were hidden. In 1600 the relics were placed in a sarcophagus sent by Clement VIII, the head being placed in a separate vessel. In 1814 the church of La Ste. Baume, wrecked during the Revolution, was restored, and in 1822 the grotto was consecrated afresh. The head of the saint now lies there, where it has lain so long, and where it has been the centre of so many pilgrimages.

—Very Rev. Hugh Pope, O.P., S.T.L.

About Anne Catherine Emmerich

Permission/Holy Cross Parish, Coesfeld, Germany

Blessed Anne Catherine Emmerich (1774-1824) was a German Augustinian nun, a mystic, stigmatist and victim soul, whose visions were copied down by Clemens Brentano (1778-1842), a poet and prominent literary figure of that time. He had paid her a visit in 1818 out of curiosity, and he remained at her bedside until she died in 1824, recording in notebooks her many, remarkable visions of the past, present and future. From 1802 until her death, she bore the wounds of the Crown of Thorns, and from 1812 the full stigmata of Our Lord, including a cross over her heart and the wound from the lance. During the last 12 years of her life, she could eat no food except Holy Communion, nor take any drink save water. She remained bed-ridden during her last 12 years, during which time she actually experienced the sufferings of Our Lord on Good Fridays and saw in vision many of the events in Biblical history. It is from these transcribed visions that Clemens Brentano himself compiled *The Dolorous Passion*, a book that has been in print almost continually since it first appeared in 1833. From his association with Sister Emmerich, Brentano returned whole-heartedly to the Catholic Faith, along with his entire family. A man of extensive learning and experience, he could nonetheless say of Anne Catherine Emmerich, "All that I have ever beheld in art or in life representative of piety, peace and innocence, sinks into insignificance compared with her." (*Life*, Vol. 1, p. 397). Anne Catherine Emmerich was declared Blessed on October 3, 2004.

SPREAD THE FAITH WITH

 TAN·BOOKS

TAN books are powerful tools for evangelization. They lift the mind to God and change lives. Millions of readers have found in TAN books and booklets an effective way to teach and defend the Faith, soften hearts, and grow in prayer and holiness of life.

Throughout history the faithful have distributed Catholic literature and sacramentals to save souls. St. Francis de Sales passed out his own pamphlets to win back those who had abandoned the Faith. Countless others have distributed the Miraculous Medal to prompt conversions and inspire deeper devotion to God. Our customers use TAN books in that same spirit.

If you have been helped by this or another TAN title, share it with others. Become a TAN Missionary and share our life changing books and booklets with your family, friends and community. We'll help by providing special discounts for books and booklets purchased in quantity for purposes of evangelization. Write or call us for additional details.

TAN Books
Attn: TAN Missionaries Department
PO Box 410437
Charlotte, NC 28241

Toll-free (800) 437-5876
missionaries@tanbooks.com

TAN · BOOKS

TAN Books was founded in 1967 to preserve the spiritual, intellectual and liturgical traditions of the Catholic Church. At a critical moment in history TAN kept alive the great classics of the Faith and drew many to the Church. In 2008 TAN was acquired by Saint Benedict Press. Today TAN continues its mission to a new generation of readers.

From its earliest days TAN has published a range of booklets that teach and defend the Faith. Through partnerships with organizations, apostolates, and mission-minded individuals, well over 10 million TAN booklets have been distributed.

More recently, TAN has expanded its publishing with the launch of Catholic calendars and daily planners—as well as Bibles, fiction, and multimedia products through its sister imprints Catholic Courses (catholiccourses.com) and Saint Benedict Press (saintbenedictpress.com).

Today TAN publishes over 500 titles in the areas of theology, prayer, devotions, doctrine, Church history, and the lives of the saints. TAN books are published in multiple languages and found throughout the world in schools, parishes, bookstores and homes.

For a free catalog, visit us online at
TANBooks.com

Or call us toll-free at
(800) 437-5876